Sentencing without Guidelines

RHYS HESTER

Sentencing without Guidelines

TEMPLE UNIVERSITY PRESS
Philadelphia • *Rome* • *Tokyo*

TEMPLE UNIVERSITY PRESS
Philadelphia, Pennsylvania 19122
tupress.temple.edu

Copyright © 2024 by Temple University—Of The Commonwealth System
 of Higher Education
All rights reserved
Published 2024

A previous version of Chapter 4 appeared as Rhys Hester, "Judicial Rotation as Centripetal Force: Sentencing in the Court Communities of South Carolina," *Criminology*, 55(1), 205–235. © 2017 American Society of Criminology.

Some passages previously appeared as "Sentencing Policies and Practices in South Carolina," *Oxford Handbook Topics in Criminology and Criminal Justice*, January 2016, Oxford University Press, https://doi.org/10.1093/oxfordhb/9780199935383.013.153. Reproduced with permission of the Licensor through PLSclear; Rhys Hester, "Punishing for the Past (Sometimes): Judicial Perspectives on Criminal History Enhancements," *The Prison Journal*, vol. 101, issue 4, pp. 443–465. © 2021 SAGE Publications. https://doi.org/10.1177/00328855211029663; and Rhys Hester, "Uniformity and Discretion: Lessons on Reform from a Failed Sentencing Guidelines Effort," *Corrections*, © 2021 by Taylor & Francis Group, LLC. DOI: 10.1080/23774657.2021.1938296.

Library of Congress Cataloging-in-Publication Data

Names: Hester, Rhys, author.
Title: Sentencing without guidelines / Rhys Hester.
Description: Philadelphia : Temple University Press, 2024. | Includes bibliographical references and index. | Summary: "This book looks to the case of South Carolina to show how its attempt to achieve sentencing uniformity through guidelines reform was successfully resisted by South Carolina judges, but how other mechanisms arose to ensure fair expectations in criminal sentencing there nonetheless"— Provided by publisher.
Identifiers: LCCN 2023044487 (print) | LCCN 2023044488 (ebook) | ISBN 9781439923542 (cloth) | ISBN 9781439923559 (paperback) | ISBN 9781439923566 (pdf)
Subjects: LCSH: Sentences (Criminal procedure)—South Carolina. | Punishment—South Carolina. | Criminal justice, Administration of—South Carolina.
Classification: LCC KFS2383.2 .H47 2024 (print) | LCC KFS2383.2 (ebook) | DDC 345.757/0772—dc23/eng/20240117
LC record available at https://lccn.loc.gov/2023044487
LC ebook record available at https://lccn.loc.gov/2023044488

♾ The paper used in this publication meets the requirements of the American National Standard for Information Sciences—Permanence of Paper for Printed Library Materials, ANSI Z39.48-1992

Printed in the United States of America

9 8 7 6 5 4 3 2 1

Dedicated to my late parents, Tommy and Lynda.

And to Pam, Eli, and Ian.

Contents

	Acknowledgments	ix
1.	Introduction	1
2.	A Brief History of Sentencing Reform	10
3.	Sentencing without Guidelines	30
4.	Judicial Rotation as Centripetal Force	58
5.	Judging Prior Record	79
6.	The Conundrum of Punishment Reform: Tension between Uniformity and Discretion	98
7.	Conclusion: Implications and Future Directions	117
	Methodological Appendix: Data, Methodologies, and Analytic Strategies	131
	Notes	143
	References	149
	Index	165

Acknowledgments

This book is the capstone to the first part of my academic career, encompassing fifteen years of my study of sentencing in South Carolina and beyond. I'm grateful for the journey so far and have a number of people to acknowledge and thank.

When I first encountered sentencing as an academic topic, I was an attorney returning to school to pursue a Ph.D. in criminology and criminal justice. I quickly gravitated toward law and punishment as a subject of interest and benefited greatly from the guidance of Dr. John Burrow, Dr. Barbara Koons-Witt, Dr. Eric Sevigny, and the late Dr. Ben Steiner, who played important roles in my education as a criminologist. They all helped shape my dissertation and early work, which became the foundation of this book.

By the time I defended my Ph.D. dissertation, I had serious sentencing fatigue and thought of abandoning the topic forever. Instead, I eventually resigned my first tenure-track position, and my family and I ventured to Minneapolis for a research fellowship in sentencing policy at the University of Minnesota Law School with the Robina Institute of Criminal Law and Criminal Justice. Although it was a nontraditional career move to leave a tenure-track job for a postdoc, those three years changed my academic trajectory and regenerated a deep affinity for studying sentencing and punishment. The most interesting work from this volume is attributable to my experiences at Robina and Minnesota Law. My time there was transformational, and I'll forever be indebted to Professors Richard Frase, Kevin Reitz, and Michael Tonry for the opportunity, experience, and inspiration.

After leaving my fellowship at Minnesota Law, I served as deputy director of the Pennsylvania Commission on Sentencing, one of the two oldest sentencing commissions in the nation, and one that remains among the most active. For a scholar who had spent the early part of my career exploring sentencing without guidelines, my time at the commission proved invaluable, allowing me to take in a fuller picture of practices under guidelines and prompting me to see nonguidelines sentencing in a new light. I'm especially grateful to the commission's indefatigable executive director, Mark Bergstrom, and to Matthew Kleiman, Leigh Tinik, Carol Zeiss, Ryan Meyers, and all of the staff, justice practitioners, and commission members I was fortunate enough to work with before leaving the commission to return to academia, this time at Clemson University.

I'm grateful to most of my colleagues at Clemson University, including my chair Dr. Katy Weisensee and dean Dr. Leslie Hossfeld, for their support. Noah Reynolds provided excellent research assistance as I finalized the manuscript. Much of this book was written while I was a visiting scholar at Penn State, and I sincerely appreciate Dr. Eric Baumer, then head of the Penn State Department of Sociology and Criminology, and Dr. Jeff Ulmer and Dr. Megan Kurlychek, director and associate director of the PSU Criminal Justice Research Center (along with the Pennsylvania Commission on Sentencing staff) for that opportunity.

I've benefited from countless interactions with judges, prosecutors, defenders, and sentencing commission members who have shared their thoughts on sentencing over the years. These conversations have shed light on court processes and decision-making and helped explain phenomena while also sparking new ideas to explore. I'm grateful for those conversations, and especially for the judges who agreed to the research interviews that much of this book are based on.

These chapters draw on several academic articles I've published in journals including *Criminology*, *Journal of Quantitative Criminology*, the *Prison Journal*, *Oxford Handbooks Online*, and *Corrections:*

Policy, Practice and Research. I would like to thank my coauthors and the editors and manuscript reviewers who provided comments and critiques and helped to improve the writing and research. Thanks also to Ryan Mulligan, editor at Temple University Press, and to his colleagues and the TUP board for their feedback and direction on the manuscript.

Finally, thank you to my wife, Pam, and boys, Eli and Ian, for the occasional support and frequent distractions from the work. I'm also especially indebted to my late parents, Tommy and Lynda, and their sacrifices for me, including my education. My father dropped out of college after two weeks but remained a voracious lover of books. He was an unwavering champion of me and (almost) all of my endeavors. I wish he could read this book, which he had such a role in making happen; his influence is on every page.

Sentencing without Guidelines

1

Introduction

Criminal punishment is the pinnacle of government power over the individual in a democratic society. We are all affected in a thousand ways by rules and regulations, but a judge pronouncing a sentence wields the power to deprive a person of their liberty, usually for years, even decades, at a time. The judge also has the authority to withhold a prison sentence and give a person a second chance. When the government gets sentencing right, it fortifies the social contract: citizens cede rights in exchange for protection, and the government provides security, reinforcing the contract when others violate the law. But when the system gets sentencing wrong, the government is a failure. Prison deprives freedom, and aside from taking life (which the government also sometimes does), there is no greater invasion into a person's life, autonomy, and dignity. The state must punish but also must attend to getting punishment right.

Because sentencing matters so much, it has received much attention. This includes the many and varied efforts at sentencing reform in the past half century in America. The scope of experimentation with major punishment structures is profound (see, e.g., Stemen et al., 2005; Tonry, 2016). Some states have abolished their parole boards, with many others restricting parole through "truth-in-sentencing"

(TIS) statutes. Jurisdictions have adopted tough-on-crime laws like three-strikes and mandatory minimum provisions that deprive judges of sentencing discretion and impose lengthy penalties as a matter of course. In more recent years, after suffering from a glut of mass incarceration, states have expanded specialty courts, like drug courts, veterans courts, and other diversionary programs, to offer second chances for some qualifying individuals. But no other reform initiative has loomed as large as sentencing guidelines.

Since the early 1980s, sentencing guidelines have been adopted by around 20 states and the federal government (Frase, 2019), as well as in a number of other countries (Hester, 2021). The leading impetus for guidelines was to impart more uniformity and fairness in sentencing. Because of the vast judicial discretion, critics claimed the U.S. sentencing system was "law without order" (Frankel, 1973). Among more general motivations for change were concerns over racial disparities in sentencing (Blumstein et al., 1983; Kramer and Ulmer, 2009; Spohn, 2000). Guidelines offered a solution by structuring sentencing, usually through a two-way matrix grid that called for tighter ranges of punishment based on (1) the seriousness of the conviction offense and (2) the defendant's prior criminal record.

South Carolina was a state on the cusp of becoming one of the earliest adopters of guidelines, but the initiative for structured sentencing reform repeatedly failed to garner the necessary political support, initially in the 1980s, then through the 1990s and into the 2000s. The story of the effort and its entropy are fascinating in their own right, as the final push for guidelines was headed by one of the most powerful political actors in the state, Republican house leader David Wilkins. As detailed in Chapter 2 of this volume, Speaker Wilkins's brother, federal judge William "Billy" Wilkins, was the first chair of the U.S. Sentencing Commission and oversaw the promulgation of federal guidelines in the 1980s. Despite Speaker Wilkins's ability to get the guidelines passed in the house, the bill never passed the state senate, and consequently South Carolina, like about half of the states, has never operated under sentencing guidelines.

As part of the now-defunct South Carolina Sentencing Commission's efforts, staff collected statewide sentencing data to develop the proposed guidelines and model their impact on the judicial and corrections systems. Those datasets were eventually discovered by faculty at the University of South Carolina's Department of Criminology and Criminal Justice, and I would become the benefactor of their existence as a Ph.D. student in search of a dissertation topic.

The South Carolina Sentencing Commission data was intriguing because it offered the promise of a rare look into sentencing practices from a state where the judges were not bound by guidelines. As I was learning in my graduate studies, the guidelines reform movement in the 1980s and 1990s spurred a proliferation of academic research on sentencing and racial disparities in punishment (see Baumer, 2013; Spohn, 2000; Ulmer, 2012). Although some more traditional ad hoc data collection efforts persisted,[1] sentencing commissions bestowed an incredible blessing to academic researchers in the form of complete annual administrative data. Scholars took full advantage of these, and scores of studies were published using the commission datasets from the federal system and the early guidelines states like Minnesota, Pennsylvania, Washington, Maryland, and Florida.

By the time I was a graduate student in the late 2000s, that era of guidelines research had established a significant presence in the discipline, but, by then, it was well-trod ground. As I began to study punishment and reform literature, I was struck by how little had been written on sentencing in the absence of guidelines, given that more than half of jurisdictions never adopted them. And it was not as though only small, unpopulated states had missed out on the guidelines movement: only two of the five most populous states, Florida and Pennsylvania, had adopted guidelines. There was a serious gap in our understanding of how people were being sentenced in much of the United States, and thus there were many unanswered questions, including concerns related to racial disparities, in a time ripe for concern over punishment practices. This gap left unknown how states without guidelines, which is most states, try to achieve a degree of fairness and predictability.

This book collects and expands on the empirical work I have conducted to uncover sentencing practices in South Carolina in an effort to shed some light on the dark area of nonguidelines sentencing. While examining sentencing in a nonguidelines state is the work's first major contribution, this research is also notable for the methodology employed. The initial phases of the project began with the traditional quantitative statistical modeling of the sentencing commission data, the results of which are detailed in Chapter 3. As that chapter conveys, the findings were surprising and spawned a second phase of research, which centered on qualitative interviews with state trial judges to get a deeper, richer account of sentencing in the state. This interview research answered calls from scholars for a return to the type of ethnographic courts research that had once been prominent in the field (Blumstein et al., 1983; Ulmer, 2012) but which had largely fallen victim to the convenience of sentencing commission data availability.

While building out the nonguidelines research presented in this book, I became immersed in other work related to sentencing guidelines and the sentencing reform movement. I embarked on the aforementioned judge interviews as a research fellow at the University of Minnesota Law School, where I was also involved in guidelines research. Minnesota was the first state to adopt sentencing guidelines, and its version of presumptive guidelines has been heralded by some as the ideal expression of sentencing guidelines (Frase, 2013).

The Minnesota Law faculty included Richard Frase, Kevin Reitz, and Michael Tonry, an unmatched triumvirate in the pantheon of sentencing policy and reform. Frase and Reitz, in particular, were champions of Minnesota-style sentencing guidelines, and under their leadership as codirectors of the Robina Institute of Criminal Law and Criminal Justice, I worked on research projects focused specifically on sentencing guidelines and punishment policy. I had come to the sentencing guidelines mecca, and it was in this context that I uncovered the most interesting findings conveyed in Chapters 5 and 6 of this volume.

My work with the Robina team was uncovering some problematic aspects of sentencing guidelines—specifically, a heavy premium placed on the defendant's criminal history (see, e.g., Frase et al., 2015; Hester, Frase, Roberts, and Mitchell, 2018). These findings from guidelines jurisdictions called to mind some of the results I was encountering in my South Carolina research. Those factors working in concert led me to explore a historical question of how the typical sentencing guidelines grid came to be in the first place. This account (which makes up part of Chapter 5) and its implications for current guidelines sentencing practices is the third major contribution of this book. As both of these projects developed, I began to see ways that guidelines jurisdictions could benefit from the findings from the nonguidelines work (and vice versa).

Thus, what began as a novel investigation of sentencing in the absence of guidelines led to some provocative implications for sentencing reform more broadly. As this volume shows, at least in this one jurisdiction, South Carolina, significant uniformity in sentencing—one of the chief objectives of the guidelines reform movement—was achieved through mechanisms other than guidelines. Further, South Carolina appeared to avoid what has emerged as a serious faux pas of guidelines jurisdictions in the overreliance on prior record in prison sentences (Hester, Frase, Roberts, and Mitchell, 2018).

Much of the sentencing reform movement distills to efforts to better achieve justice as defined by the Aristotelian maxim: treat like cases alike and different cases differently. There are lessons to be learned from South Carolina.

Uniformity and Discretion

A central premise of this volume is that tools to achieve justice (treating like cases alike and different cases differently) can come in unexpected forms. Familiar tools like sentencing guidelines offer progress but not a cure for sentencing problems, and mechanisms beyond guidelines may help to advance the ends of justice. Few areas of law and policy have realized as much potential to serve as Justice Louis Brandeis's state "laboratories" for policy experimentation as punishment and sentencing (Reitz, 2009). But when the research field is dominated by a key feature selection (i.e., guidelines), the potential value of these experiments is not fully realized. If sentencing research only comes from sentencing guidelines jurisdictions, then science will never be informed by the results of the other experiments currently going on in the majority of U.S. jurisdictions. It is critical that the field expand sentencing research beyond sentencing guidelines jurisdictions.

The serendipity of South Carolina's failed guidelines efforts and accompanying data provided the rare opportunity to examine sentencing in a nonguidelines state. The lessons are insightful, even for guidelines jurisdictions. As the chapters in this volume show, South

Carolina was able to achieve many of the goals of sentencing reform without sentencing guidelines. It has done this through other mechanisms, including the retention of a once-ubiquitous but now-vestige practice of judicial rotation in which judges travel across many counties to hold court. These findings (detailed in Chapter 4) highlight both structural and cultural ways that this state has achieved the objectives of sentencing reform without the primary formal changes most often associated with reform. Some of these lessons could be adapted by other jurisdictions, even guidelines jurisdictions, to help advance the enduring goals of uniformity, fairness, and legitimacy in sentencing.

Further, the findings from South Carolina provide insight into some harmful unintended consequences of sentencing guidelines in the form of robust prior record enhancements. Guidelines formulize the role of prior convictions by scoring aspects of crime involvement (e.g., number of prior juvenile offenses, misdemeanors, felonies, and custody violations, often with scores weighting more serious offenses with greater points). These criminal history points are then translated into higher punishment recommendations. The approach has some serious unintended consequences. Frase (2009) found that a full two-thirds of the racial disparities in Minnesota sentencing were attributable to the operation of the guideline criminal history score. Further work by Frase and Hester (2019) found that considerable portions of racial disparities in sentencing in other guidelines jurisdictions were also attributable to guideline prior record scores. In addition, prior record enhancements end up expanding prison bed space requirements with nonviolent and aging individuals and disrupt efforts at punishment proportionality when lower-severity defendants serve more time than higher-severity defendants (Hester, Frase, Roberts, and Mitchell, 2018; Frase and Roberts, 2019; see also Ostrom et al., 2008).

The results from South Carolina suggested that judges, in the absence of guideline influence, did not view prior record as having a formulaic, monotonic association with increased punishment. The historical case study that this finding inspired (relayed in Chapter 5) shows that those rules were incorporated to establish a single grid tool for ease of administration. Perhaps unwittingly, these decisions would lead to the collateral consequences of racial disparities and longer prison sentences for some aging and nonviolent individuals. These findings bolster a message for sentencing commissions to revisit and revise their guidelines—insights that would not have been realized without a program of scholarship aimed at an understudied nonguidelines state.

Punishment and Court Culture

This book is situated within literatures that attempt to understand (1) why individuals get the criminal sentences they do and (2) how legal reform mechanisms (like guidelines, among others) can influence punishment goals and policy. The chapters contribute to several theoretical areas, including focal concerns theory, implicit bias, courts as communities theory, the theory of inhabited institutions, and neo-institutional theory. These theories make up the core guiding framework for understanding how individuals get sentenced, how racial disparities emerge in sentencing outcomes, and how local court cultures (and broader statewide court cultures) can influence punishment.

According to the focal concerns theory, judges and court actors have three central concerns when sentencing: assessing the blameworthiness of the defendant, protecting public safety, and considering other practical constraints (like the availability of jail space) (Steffensmeier and Painter-Davis, 2018; Ulmer, 2012). Through related theoretical mechanisms like uncertainty avoidance, causal attribution, and implicit bias, focal concerns theory postulates how court actors might be influenced by extralegal characteristics like race. The courts as communities and inhabited institutions perspectives offer a broader look at the inner workings of courts and the external political, social, and economic influences that might affect outcomes (Ulmer, 2019). Key to these theories is the notion of local legal culture, the idea that each local court organization (usually thought of at the county court level) develops its own set of norms of case processing and outcomes, including sentencing preferences.

These notions of distinct court communities and the resultant geographically based sentencing preferences are especially important to this volume because they provide the theoretical foundation for a concern over disparate sentencing practices that sentencing guidelines were designed to address. Studies from guidelines jurisdictions continue to find geographic differences attributable to the varied ways local court cultures adapt to or circumvent aspects of sentencing reform innovations like guidelines (see Chapter 3). Against this backdrop, an initial expectation was that outcomes in South Carolina would be especially divergent across counties since no guidelines existed to normalize sentencing to any degree. This expectation is shattered in Chapter 3 and then in Chapter 4 gives rise to some broader theoretical adaptations related to the circuit rotation and statewide culture, which constitute key contributions of this work.

While these theories help to situate the core findings from this mixed-methods study, the final chapters of the volume turn to two additional theories in the hope of advancing an agenda for all jurisdictions to consider research from both guidelines and nonguidelines studies to reevaluate the policy means for achieving the end goals of sentencing reform. Neoinstitutional theory helps situate what sentencing guidelines jurisdictions can learn from the findings from this nonguidelines research. Neoinstitutionalism contemplates several mechanisms for achieving organizational uniformity, which, in this context, translates to the sentencing reform goal of sentencing uniformity (see Ulmer, 2019). One mechanism is coercive isomorphism. ("Isomorphism" refers to similarity or uniformity, so "coercive isomorphism" refers to creating similarity through coercive means.) Superimposing new formal legal rules like sentencing guidelines is an example of an attempt to achieve uniformity with a coercive tool. However, uniformity can also be achieved through mimetic and normative isomorphism (uniformity achieved through mimicry or informal cultural forces rather than coercive ones). The South Carolina results demonstrate this ability and present some ideas on how sentencing commissions and reformers can consider mimetic and normative isomorphism tools to increase uniformity, with or without guidelines.

Outline of the Book

This volume proceeds with Chapter 2, which sets the context of the national sentencing reform movement from the 1970s through the 2020s. The chapter provides an overview of the history of South Carolina's reform efforts, including the story of the Wilkins brothers, and provides a sketch of the modified indeterminant sentencing structure that operates in the wake of the guidelines movement's failures. Chapter 3 presents a defendant-level study of sentencing in South Carolina. It provides the baseline statistical findings using the defunct sentencing commission dataset of over 17,000 defendants. The chapter frames the findings in focal concerns theory and elaborates on issues of racial disparities in sentencing. Chapter 3 also addresses the broader influences of individual judges and the social, political, and economic influences of geographic location. Drawing on the courts as communities and related frameworks, this chapter sets up the dominant expectations of widespread interjudge and geographical differences in sentencing but curiously finds a great degree of uniformity in sentencing despite the lack of guidelines. To probe further for answers, the project turned to qualitative interviews of trial court judges, the results of which are presented in Chapters 4 and 5. Chapter 4 focuses on the impact of judicial rotation and the novel concept of the "plea judge," which rotation creates. In Chapter 5, the specific role of prior record in sentencing is analyzed—one of the starkest contrasts between the findings from the South Carolina work and research from guidelines jurisdictions. Chapter 6 considers how these findings from South Carolina translate into policy takeaways for other jurisdictions, including guideline jurisdictions. This chapter also offers original research on guideline departures in Minnesota, calling into question the degree to which guidelines have fully addressed the tension between treating like cases alike and different cases differently. The chapter provides both a theoretical framework for applying some of the lessons from South Carolina and some concrete ideas for translating these lessons into policy. Chapter 7 concludes the volume with final thoughts on sentencing reform, the utility of guidelines, and the ongoing effort to realize the Aristotelian ideal of achieving greater uniformity in sentencing while preserving the discretion to treat different cases differently.

2

A Brief History of Sentencing Reform

This chapter sketches a brief history of the sentencing reform movement in the United States and explains how the legal framework of South Carolina fits within that larger story. The state is characterized by an indeterminate system in which judges continue to exercise considerable discretion, though that discretion has been curbed through statutory maximums and mandatory minimums. A parole board still operates, though parole eligibility is subject to an array of rules that require an offender to serve a minimum of 25 percent, 33 percent, or 85 percent of their imposed sentence, depending on the offense. In addition, South Carolina retains the practice of judicial rotation, whereby state trial judges travel, holding court in various counties throughout the state. A central part of the South Carolina story involves the failed guidelines effort. South Carolina was among the earliest states to consider sentencing guidelines, with considerations going back to the 1970s, before even Minnesota and Pennsylvania (the first guidelines states) promulgated structured sentencing. The state's efforts also have an interesting connection to the prominent federal guidelines. The chair of the inaugural U.S. Sentencing Commission was federal judge and South Carolina lawyer Billy Wilkins, who had been President Ronald Reagan's first judicial appointment to the federal bench. As Judge Wilkins was leading the federal guidelines movement, his brother David Wilkins was rising through the ranks of the South Carolina political machine. He soon became Speaker of the South Carolina House of Representatives and took over the South Carolina guidelines efforts, also serving as the chair of the South Carolina Sentencing Commission. Despite his influence, judicial opposition to guidelines prevented their adoption, and after decades of effort, the guidelines movement eventually died of exhaustion. Nevertheless, the commission played an important role in the state's punishment reform, including through a major reorganization of the criminal code, TIS legislation, and—critically for this work—through the collection of data to model the impact of the proposed guidelines. This latter effort left a legacy dataset of statewide sentencing outcomes from a nonguidelines state, making it possible to address a considerable gap in the literature.

Sentencing Reform in South Carolina

The past few decades of sentencing policy reform in South Carolina unfold as a story of almosts and half measures. Many parts of the story are what outside observers might expect: a highly carceral southern state that led the nation in per capita imprisonment for much of the 1980s and 1990s—one of the most punitive states in the most punitive nation during the most punitive decades of the modern era. But other aspects of the South Carolina account might surprise observers. In 1977 the state was actually poised to be an early progressive leader in sentencing reform.

In the late 1970s, several influential judges began work on guidelines through an ad hoc judicial "sentencing guidelines committee." Representatives, including South Carolina Supreme Court Justice David Harwell—a spearhead of the guidelines movement—visited the newly formed Minnesota Sentencing Guidelines Commission in the early 1980s and returned to South Carolina intent on creating a new sentencing structure on the presumptive guidelines model developed there. The ad hoc committee was transformed into a legislatively enacted guidelines commission in the early 1980s. The commission developed guidelines, but they were not adopted, and in 1987 the legislature abolished the commission. However, a few years later, the commission made a return under the leadership of political up-and-comer David Wilkins (brother of the newly minted federal judge William Wilkins, who at the same time was shaping the federal guidelines in their formative stages as the first chair of the U.S. Sentencing Commission). David Wilkins led a guidelines effort that spanned from the late 1980s up through the early 2000s but that never achieved its ultimate goal. In the end, a variety of state leaders labored across parts of four decades to pass sentencing guidelines—efforts that, ultimately, were in vain.

Guidelines never passed, but the several iterations of guidelines commissions did influence sentencing reform in the state. The commission of the 1990s and early 2000s collected statewide sentencing data that has provided the rare opportunity to empirically examine sentencing practices statewide in a jurisdiction that does not have guidelines but maintains parole release discretion for most offenders. Virtually all of the statewide sentencing data that has served as the basis for sentencing research over the past several decades has been in the form of secondary administrative data collected by sentencing commissions in states with sentencing guidelines. Thus, through the historical accident of the South Carolina Sentencing Commission's failed efforts at guidelines, the state's data provide a unique look into the practices and patterns of sentencing in a jurisdiction where judges still retain tremendous discretion over the sentences imposed on offenders—research discussed in Chapter 3.

South Carolina is one of a number of states that has experienced some mitigation in prison growth since the 2000s. For South Carolina, the decline in prison rates began around 2001, which was earlier than most states. The decline likely flowed from the budgetary constraints that accompanied the 2001 recession, which were exacerbated after the economic collapse of 2008. The state also took formal measures to curtail prison growth with a comprehensive crime bill that took effect in 2010. The law expands parole eligibility for many drug crimes, mandates risk and needs assessments for probationers and parolees, and requires administrative intermediate sanctions for supervision violators, among other things. Post-2020, the prison-rate trajectories look promising, and perhaps the state has found a way—through serendipitous structural characteristics and informal policy reactions, coupled with a new wave of smart-on-crime reform—to temper the punitiveness of earlier eras.

Sentencing Restructured: Reform Nationwide and in South Carolina, 1975–2015

Many U.S. jurisdictions have engaged in significant sentencing policy reform since the 1970s. Sentencing reform has been part of the legislative agenda in South Carolina for decades. However, as this section outlines, as of the 2020s the state still looks much more like the traditional indeterminate system than many of its sister states. South Carolina continues to use parole (though in a more restricted form than the pure indeterminate model) and operates without guidelines, though judges are constrained by certain mandatory minimum penalties, and the system as a whole reflects the strong influence of the war on drugs. After outlining these structural guideposts, this section provides a historical analysis of the several iterations of the state's sentencing commissions, including their motivations, successes, and failures.

The National Context of Sentencing Reform

Like those in most states, South Carolina sentencing laws and practices have undergone tremendous reform since the 1970s, though the changes were not as sweeping as in some jurisdictions. For the first three-quarters of the 1900s, all U.S. jurisdictions operated under indeterminate sentencing systems in which judges enjoyed wide discretion in making front-end sentencing decisions and parole boards had broad authority over the back-end decisions of when to release offenders (Tonry, 1996; Rhine, 2012). By the 1970s, crime was on the rise, concerns over disparities and discretion were elevated, and faith in the rehabilitative potential of prison was dwindling (Martinson, 1974; Wilson, 1975). The sentencing and punishment landscape was ripe for change. The impetus for sentencing reform came from multiple fronts, including progressive concerns over fairness, equity, and racial disparities in sentencing (Davis, 1969; Frankel, 1973; von Hirsch, 1976) and a growing emphasis on crime control (see Feeley and Simon, 1992; Marvell and Moody, 1996; Wilson, 1975). Around this time, the United States also entered the "get-tough-on-crime" era, in which social and cultural sensibilities resulting from the normalization of high crime rates led to increasingly punitive attitudes on the part of the public and policymakers (Garland, 2000, 2012). As a result of this confluence of social and political forces, jurisdictions adopted a variety of reforms related to sentencing and punishment; the most substantial initiatives can be categorized into four areas: (1) whether the jurisdiction has adopted sentencing guidelines; (2) whether it has abolished parole release discretion or adopted TIS; (3) how extensively the jurisdiction has adopted tough-on-crime initiatives, including mandatory minimums, three-strikes laws, and life without parole provisions; and (4) how zealously it has engaged in the war on drugs (for extensive reviews of these initiatives, see Travis, Western, and Redburn, 2014, chap. 4; Stemen, Rengifo, and Wilson, 2005; Tonry, 1996). The following paragraphs discuss the current legal landscape in South Carolina as defined by these primary sentencing features.

The Current Structure of Sentencing in South Carolina

South Carolina continues to retain parole release discretion, though in a more constrained form than the pure indeterminate model of the 1970s and earlier. Judges continue to exercise large grants of discretion, free from the constraints of guidelines. In addition, as in many states, South Carolina law reflects the usual suspects of the get-tough movement—including mandatory minimums, TIS, and three-strikes laws. And overall the state substantially ramped up arrests, prosecutions, and punishment as it waged the war on drugs. This section also discusses other aspects of the South Carolina judicial system that are critical to its current operation, even though they are not part of the story of sentencing reform. These include the continued practice of having trial judges routinely travel (rather than hold court in just one county), selecting judges through legislative appointment, and, until recently, maintaining prosecutorial control over trial dockets.

Parole Release Retention
The parole board, housed in the South Carolina Department of Probation, Parole and Pardon Services (SCDPPP), comprises seven members appointed by the governor for six-year terms and subject to senate approval (S.C. Code Ann. Section 24-21-10[B]; SCDPPP, 2022). One of several rules may apply for parole eligibility depending on the classification of the conviction offense. As a baseline, many prisoners are eligible for parole after serving just 25 percent of their sentence. (While

eligible after serving 25 percent, most of these offenders serve more like 55 percent to 65 percent of their sentence, with the early release attributed to good-time credit; Crooks, 2015.) Statutorily defined "violent" offenders must serve at least one-third of their sentence, unless also subject to the more stringent 85 percent rule from the 1996 TIS legislation, which applies to any crime carrying a maximum term of 20 years or more. Finally, a few offenses carry special parole eligibility restrictions. Examples include absolutely no parole for murder (offenders must serve 100 percent of their sentence) and a literal minimum of at least seven years for armed robbery (Deutschmann and Benjamin, 2000).

While guidelines never materialized, in the 1990s the sentencing commission was successful in implementing TIS legislation. Although initially aimed at all crimes with a maximum penalty of a year or more in prison, the bill that passed was limited, requiring offenders sentenced for an offense with a maximum penalty of 20 years or more to serve at least 85 percent of their sentence before being eligible for parole (Act No. 83, 1995 Acts 545; South Carolina Sentencing Guidelines Commission [SCSGC], 2001). A more encompassing TIS package failed over concerns that without guidelines to complement parole reductions, the already-overcrowded prison system would become grossly unmanageable (Ghent, 1998; Harwell-Beach, 1998; SCSGC, 2001).

Tough-on-Crime Initiatives

In addition to TIS, further get-tough initiatives included mandatory minimums and a three-strikes law. Most of these mandatory minimum offenses sought to impose stricter punishment for gun and drug crimes (Ghent, 1998; McAninch et al., 2013; McCulley, 1999; SCSGC, n.d.). In South Carolina, these include lengthy minimums of up to 25 years for many trafficking offenses (McAninch et al., 2013 McCulley, 1999). As reported in Chapter 3, in 2001 there were 34 separate offense codes subject to a nonsuspendible mandatory minimum penalty.

Taken together, the parole eligibility rules, TIS, and mandatory penalties mean that while South Carolina never abolished parole, it also is no longer a mirror image of the traditional indeterminate system (see Reitz, 1998, 2012; Rothman, 1980). Still, for many offenses, parole is possible after service of just 25 percent of the sentence, making

South Carolina's hybrid indeterminacy an important aspect of its sentencing structure.

Prison Release Discretion
Another meaningful outlet for early release comes from the South Carolina Department of Corrections (DOC) in the form of good-time and early release credits. University of Minnesota Law professor Kevin Reitz and colleagues (2023) have developed a comprehensive comparison of the varying degrees of indeterminacy among U.S. states. As they describe in their report on South Carolina, the state operates with a "high degree of indeterminancy," meaning that many individuals could get released after serving 20 percent to 40 percent of their sentence. They note that the South Carolina DOC is "especially powerful" because the DOC can award time credits that reduce the parole board's release discretion. These credits include good-time credits, which can accrue as much has 20 days for each month (a 40 percent reduction) served in faithful observance of the rules of the institution. Even violent "no parole" offenders can earn three days per month, almost a 10 percent reduction on their sentence. Individuals can also earn work credits and education credits. Those credits can reach 180 days per year for most inmates and 72 days per year for no parole individuals, with some violent crime offenders able to earn work credits but not education credits. (Some exclusions apply: individuals serving life sentences or 30-year minimums for murder are not eligible for these credits.) According to Reitz and colleagues, these credits reduce an inmate's maximum prison term. Thus, while they are still eligible for parole, the generous earned-time credits allow an inmate to reduce their prison time without reliance on the parole board. Reitz and colleagues (2023) observe that the state has "an unusually generous credit system" that "may be the largest of any state."

The Judicial System
In addition to the foregoing reform initiatives, several aspects of the South Carolina judicial system are critical to the ultimate shaping of its sentencing patterns and practices. These include judicial rotation (or traveling judges) and the legislative selection of judges, among others.

South Carolina's judicial system is organized by the state's 46 counties, grouped into 16 judicial circuits. A chief prosecutor, known as a solicitor, is selected through popular partisan elections to serve each circuit. South Carolina was the only state in the nation where prosecutors continued to control the docket until 2012, when a state supreme court case, *State v. Langford*, declared that the practice was an unconstitutional violation of the separation of powers (see also Siegel, 2005). The courts of general jurisdiction are known as circuit courts, and the circuit judges are selected by the legislature. (Virginia is the only other state with a legislative appointment of trial judges.)

A particularly noteworthy characteristic of the court system is the continued practice of trial judge rotation throughout the various counties and circuits. Judges in South Carolina do not sit exclusively in one court but instead rotate in and out of different counties throughout the year, a practice mandated by the state constitution (S.C. Constitution, Art. V, s 14). Rotation is implemented ad hoc through order of the chief justice. Judges spend much of their time in their home circuit, with rotation occurring frequently but nonsystematically. In fiscal year 2001, judges traveled to an average of 12 counties, and counties saw an average of 13 judges rotating through during the year (with a range of 5 to 33 different judges in one county; Hester and Sevigny, 2016). Currently, around 50 full-time active circuit judges hear cases in the general jurisdiction courts, making the ratio of judges to the general population one of the lowest in the nation. (According to Schauffler, et al. [2006], South Carolina had approximately 1.1 general jurisdiction judges per 100,000 in the general population; the national average was around 4 per 100,000.)

Caseload burdens are concomitantly among the greatest in the country. Plea bargaining is the predominant way of conducting business in South Carolina courtrooms. In 2001 over 98 percent of offenders were sentenced after a guilty plea as opposed to a trial (see Chapter 3). Pleas in South Carolina take one of three forms: (1) a straight plea, where the defendant pleads guilty with no recommendation from the prosecution; (2) a recommended plea, where the prosecutor offers a recommendation that has no binding effect on the judge or outcome; or (3) a negotiated plea, which is presented to the judge as an agreed-upon outcome by the parties that the judge must either accept or reject.

There are no statistics on how frequently these different methods of guilty pleas occur.

Also noteworthy is that South Carolina judges virtually never make use of a presentence investigation report. There is a mechanism for requesting a report from the probation department, but it is only rarely used by a small number of judges. South Carolina judges typically pronounce the sentence upon conviction or plea; on the rare occasion a presentencing report is requested, by the time it is prepared and delivered, the presiding judge is likely holding court in a different county. Further, judges are aware of the additional work the reports place on probation officers. In this heavily overburdened jurisdiction, presentence reports have simply never been integrated into the sentencing process (Richards, 1986; Hester, 2017).

Appellate review of sentences is extremely restricted. As explained in *State v. Goodall*, "It is the established rule in this state that this court has no jurisdiction on appeal to correct a sentence alleged to be excessive, when it is within the limits prescribed by law for the discretion of the trial judge, and is not the result of partiality, prejudice, oppression, or corrupt motive" (internal quotation marks and citations omitted). (See also *In re MBH*, "A trial judge has broad discretion in sentencing within statutory limits. A judge must be permitted to consider any and all information that reasonably might bear on the proper sentence for a particular defendant. A sentence will not be overturned absent an abuse of discretion when the ruling is based on an error of law or a factual conclusion without evidentiary support.")

While the modifications to parole eligibility, the proliferation of mandatory minimums, and the execution of the war on drugs have left an undeniable mark on South Carolina sentencing policy, the leading headline in the state's sentencing story is the perennial reform failure: the decades-long initiative to adopt sentencing guidelines. Central to the guidelines struggle were four distinct manifestations of sentencing guidelines commissions.

The Laborings and Legacies of the Sentencing Commissions

The end result of reform efforts in South Carolina is much simpler than its long and convoluted history of initiatives would suggest. Many of the policies discussed earlier were facilitated through the work of several sentencing guidelines commissions. Accordingly, the commissions' work cannot be viewed as a total failure; in fact, the commission of the 1990s helped usher in some of the most important policy changes to South Carolina's criminal law and punishment system. However, despite heroic efforts that spanned decades, the foremost goal of the commissions—to see sentencing guidelines come into effect—never materialized. Rather, the efforts, which began in the 1970s and persisted through the 1980s and 1990s, finally died from exhaustion in the 2000s.

For a time, South Carolina was poised to be on the forefront of progressive sentencing reform. As far back as 1965, South Carolina Judge Francis Nicholson had raised concerns about sentencing practices (Richards, 1986; Toliver and Brown, 1974). In the early 1970s, the state's Criminal Justice Division commissioned Professors William McAninch and Eldon Wedlock of the University of South Carolina School of Law to review and evaluate the state's criminal code and sentencing practices. Among other things, their report raised concerns over unjustified disparities, the lack of presentence investigation reports, and the need for a separate sentencing hearing and appellate review of sentences (Richards, 1986). While the McAninch and Wedlock report did not gain traction among lawmakers, a second sentencing report, facilitated through the South Carolina Bar, which largely mirrored the recommendations of the McAninch and Wedlock report, caught the attention of several influential officeholders, including South Carolina Chief Justice Woodrow Lewis. In 1977, Chief Justice Lewis and four other interested judges (including a trial judge named David Harwell) formed a group that, in time, became an ad hoc judicial sentencing committee.

This Circuit Court Sentencing Guidelines Committee created a set of proposed guidelines intended to impart greater uniformity in sentencing. (In addition to this committee, there were three subsequent permutations of sentencing guidelines commissions and most recently a sentencing reform commission, which did not consider guidelines but is discussed at the end of this chapter; these various commissions are listed in Table 2.1 along with the years in which they operated and their major efforts and achievements.) By 1981 Judge Harwell had become South Carolina Supreme Court Justice Harwell. In that year, he and court administration staffer Anderson Surles (who also served

TABLE 2.1. SUMMARY OF SOUTH CAROLINA SENTENCING COMMISSIONS

Commission Title	Years Active	Summary of Activity
Circuit Court Sentencing Guidelines Committee	1977–1982	Worked on sample guidelines; sent delegates to the Minnesota Sentencing Guidelines Commission
Executive Sentencing Guidelines Commission	1982–1983	Created a proposal for presumptive guidelines and a permanent, independent sentencing commission, similar to Minnesota's
Harwell Sentencing Guidelines Commission	1983–1987	Proposed a crime reclassification system and advisory guidelines, which were submitted to the legislature in 1985 but never adopted
Wilkins Sentencing Guidelines Commission	1989–2004	Succeeded in implementing crime reclassification and truth-in-sentencing; received funding for data collection and prison simulation modeling; introduced guidelines bills on several occasions, which twice passed the house but never received a vote in the senate
Sentencing Reform Commission	2008–2010	Did not consider guidelines but was responsible for a comprehensive omnibus act in 2010

Note: The names given to the commissions (e.g., Executive, Harwell, Wilkins) are not official; each iteration of the commission was simply referred as the "sentencing guidelines commission"; the titles are supplied by the author to help the reader distinguish among the different iterations.

as an assistant to the guidelines committee and who would later become the executive director of the legislatively formed guidelines commission) traveled to Minnesota, a state that had recently promulgated presumptive sentencing guidelines (Richards, 1986). Harwell and Surles returned to South Carolina convinced that replicating the Minnesota model—complete with its permanent and independent sentencing commission and presumptively binding sentencing guidelines—was the best way forward for sentencing reform in South Carolina. The ad hoc sentencing committee continued to push forward with attempts to construct and field-test sample guidelines but was hampered by "procedural and logistical disputes among the judiciary" (Richards, 1986).

A legislatively created sentencing commission would be forthcoming, but Governor Richard Riley chose to create one by executive order in January 1982 to maintain the reform momentum (Executive Order No. 82-12). The order cited concerns over (1) equity and sentencing disparities; (2) the need for formal guidelines to assist judges in determining appropriate sentences; (3) the lack of an offense classification system in the state; and (4) the desire for a rational and consistent sentencing structure that would reduce disparities and ensure proportionality in punishment, guided by the severity of the offense and the prior criminal history of the offender.

This Executive Sentencing Commission included 18 members from various branches of the government and the public. According to M. S. Richards (1986), the commission divided work among three committees and was productive in hashing out key formational issues regarding what the commission and guidelines should look like. Among other things, the various committees decided that a court of appeals was needed to review sentencing appeals; that crimes should be reclassified into streamlined, cohesive categories; that the minimum sentence served prior to parole eligibility should be raised to 60 percent; and that a permanent and independent sentencing commission should exist and should be composed of representatives from all three branches of government. The guidelines were discussed as "presumptive," though some on the commission preferred advisory guidelines. Richards (1986, p. 57) summarized the executive commission's work as follows:

> A presumptive range of fixed sentences was based on an appropriate combination of offense seriousness and offender characteristics. Impositions outside the presumptive limits were required to have written reasons; moreover, those decisions were subject to appellate review. The proposed guidelines were to weigh existing current sentencing and release procedures before instituting proposed reforms. Correctional resources (State and local) also were to be taken into consideration.

Thomas L. Hughston, Jr. and Dill Blackwell were both state representatives and commission members; in 1983 they introduced a bill that eventually created a permanent legislative sentencing commission (the

Harwell Sentencing Guidelines Commission, Table 2.1) to supersede the executive one. The new commission consisted of 13 voting members and 4 nonvoting members, all to serve four-year terms. Though the draft bill initially spoke of a "presumptive range," the final mandate replaced "presumptive" with "advisory."[1] By mid-1983 this new Harwell Sentencing Guidelines Commission was instituted and meeting. However, a turnover in membership from the executive to the legislative commission rendered null some of the consensus built by the former. "Many of the old controversies were revived and this hindered the Commission's work" (Richards, 1986, p. 63).

Eventually the Harwell Sentencing Guidelines Commission endorsed a crime reclassification system and developed grid-based advisory guidelines. Judges would be allowed to sentence outside the guidelines' recommendations but would be required to state their reasons for doing so. By the beginning of 1985, the guidelines package was prepared for legislative consideration. But as of June 1986, the legislature had "yet to act favorably upon this well-considered set of proposals" (Richards, 1986, p. 68). In fact, the 1986 legislature did not fund the commission for the upcoming year, and in 1987 the commission was repealed, though its hiatus would be short-lived (SCSGC, 2001).

Interestingly, as the commission suffered this initial failure, a former South Carolina trial judge was front and center in the formulation of the federal guidelines. Before becoming a circuit court judge, William W. Wilkins had been a prosecutor and, earlier in his career, an aide to the storied Senator Strom Thurmond (who, depending on the party in power, was longtime chair or minority leader of the U.S. Senate Judiciary Committee). In 1981 Judge Wilkins became President Ronald Reagan's first appointment to the federal bench. He was rumored to be a candidate for director of the Federal Bureau of Investigation, and while he did not get that post, after the Sentencing Reform Act of 1984 created the U.S. Sentencing Commission, Judge Wilkins was appointed as its first chair. He led the commission through the development and implementation of the guidelines and continued as its chair for almost 10 years, during which time he was also confirmed to the Fourth Circuit Court of Appeals (Hester, 2016).

While Judge Wilkins was shepherding the vastly unpopular federal guidelines through their nascent years (they went into effect November 1, 1987), his younger brother David H. Wilkins, a rising star in South Carolina's Republican Party, was rekindling the South Carolina guidelines flame as chair of the state's House Judiciary Committee. David Wilkins introduced legislation that reinstituted the briefly defunct commission and served as chair of the new commission.

The 1989 Wilkins Sentencing Guidelines Commission looked much like its predecessor, with 13 voting members, 4 nonvoting members, and a legislative mandate to propose advisory guidelines. Justice Harwell continued for a time as the representative from the supreme court, and Anderson Surles of court administration continued for a short time as director. Importantly, Chair Wilkins would serve as a constant presence for more than a decade.

The Wilkins Commission reintroduced advisory guidelines and got back to work on crime reclassification, which was seen as a necessary first step to laying the groundwork for guidelines. David Wilkins was an influential chair, and his leadership undoubtedly accounted for any success the commission would see over the next decade. Wilkins would soon become Speaker of the House (and eventually U.S. ambassador to Canada under President George W. Bush). He introduced a crime reclassification bill (H.3400), which passed the house in 1991 but was vetoed by Republican Governor Carroll Campbell in 1993. Wilkins then introduced a new classification bill (H.3151), which Governor Campbell eventually signed into law, finally establishing order to what the Harwell Commission had described as a "hodgepodge system of grouping criminal offenses" (SCSGC, 1991). The Crime Reclassification Act reorganized over 700 offenses into six felony and three misdemeanor categories; very serious crimes such as murder were designated as exempt from classification (SCSGC, 1997). A new advisory guidelines bill, tweaked to account for the reclassification, was introduced in 1993 but was apparently met with cold support by those outside Wilkins's reach of influence in the house. Worse, government restructuring had been a cornerstone of Governor Campbell's campaign, and by 1993 he made good on his promises with a major restructuring bill that, among many other things, would repeal the sentencing commission effective July 1, 1994.

Although crime reclassification was a feather in the cap, it fell far short of the goal, well over 10 years going, to create sentencing guidelines in South Carolina. Speaker Wilkins hired Ashley Harwell—his former law clerk at the House Judiciary Committee and the niece to the now-retired chief justice and guidelines champion David Harwell—as executive director to shut down the commission. However, fortuitously, the Edna McConnell Clark Foundation took an interest in the guidelines efforts in South Carolina around this time. The Clark Foundation's State-Centered Program was charged with assisting "state policymakers and criminal justice leaders interested in controlling the growth of prison populations without compromising public safety" by helping officials undertake policy analysis and engage stakeholders in exploring how to use criminal justice resources more effectively (Clark Foundation, 2022; Hester, 2016). The Clark Foundation encouraged the commission to apply for grant funding to collect data and construct simulation models to demonstrate how proposed policy changes related to guidelines and parole eligibility might affect key outcomes (SCSGC, n.d.; Wilkins, 2015).

With Wilkins's considerable political capital and the unexpected funding opportunity, the commission ducked the government restructuring repeal. In 1994, rather than closing its doors as originally slated, the commission experienced what it viewed as a partial victory with the passage of TIS legislation. As adopted, TIS applied only to offenders with sentences of 20 years or more, who would now be required to serve a minimum of 85 percent of their sentence (SCSGC, 1997; McAninch et al., 2013). The original TIS legislation would have applied to any crime with a maximum penalty of a year or more, but it was cut back over concerns that without controlling the number of offenders entering the system on the front end, such back-end constraints would have a detrimental impact on an already-bulging prison system. This concern, according to the commission's 1997 report, "created renewed interest in the concept of sentencing guidelines," and the legislature requested the development of guidelines that would complement a more comprehensive TIS package (SCSGC, 1997).

Armed with funding from the Edna McConnell Clark Foundation, the commission collected sentencing data from around the state, developed simulation models, and proposed a newly revised set of guidelines. Speaker Wilkins introduced the 1997 guidelines bill (H.3842), which passed the house in 1998 but which never received a vote in the senate. The guidelines were reintroduced in 1999 (H.3108) and again passed the house but, also again, never received a vote in the senate.

The commission continued to collect data in the early 2000s, but eventually it became clear that the guidelines effort lacked political support outside Speaker Wilkins's formidable shadow of influence in the house. While technically never repealed, the commission was not funded after fiscal year 2004. In 2005 President George W. Bush nominated, and the Senate confirmed, Speaker Wilkins for Ambassador to Canada; by then, the guidelines movement had surrendered to atrophy.

Imprisonment Decline

This final section discusses more recent changes in South Carolina sentencing policies and practices. A comprehensive 2010 Crime Act sought to reduce prison growth while maintaining public safety. This section describes the most important parts of that 2010 act and provides some preliminary assessment on the impact of the new law. However, a formal change in law is not the only way to influence criminal justice outcomes, as a review of the prison trends in South Carolina reveals. Court actors are entrusted with large grants of discretion; they are also embedded within court communities subject to social, economic, and political pressures from outside influences. These actors shape and reshape policy and outcomes quite apart from formal changes in law.

Omnibus Crime Reduction and Sentencing Reform Act of 2010

The most recent development in South Carolina sentencing came with the passage of the Omnibus Crime Reduction and Sentencing Reform Act of 2010 (the 2010 Crime Act). The origins of the 2010 Crime Act came with a 2008 act that created the Sentencing Reform Commission (see Table 2.1), which was tasked with recommending reforms "to make South Carolina better and safer; reduce recidivism and the revolving door to prisons; propose fair and effective sentencing options; use tax dollars wisely; and improve public safety by ensuring that prison beds are available for violent offenders who need to be in prison and remain in prison" (South Carolina Sentencing Reform Commission, 2010, p. 1). Although the enabling legislation contained a misguided reference to the commission reviewing and recommending "appropriate changes to current sentencing guidelines," the 2010 Reform Commission never seriously considered reentering the guidelines fray.

The motivation behind the 2010 Reform Commission was concern over "rising recidivism rates, increasing prison populations, limited sentencing alternatives and re-entry programs, and mounting correctional costs" (South Carolina Sentencing Reform Commission, 2010, p. 1). The most substantial aspects of the final legislation were (1) expanding parole eligibility for numerous drug possession, manufacture, and distribution offenses; (2) requiring the SCDPPP to develop policies related to risk and needs assessments for probationers and parolees; (3) requiring a minimum of 180 days of reentry supervision for certain offender classifications (many offenders had been choosing to max out their prison terms to avoid parole supervision); and (4) establishing procedures for administrative intermediate sanctions for probation and parole violations. The legislation also removed the disparity between crack and powder cocaine sentencing.

In 2012 the SCDPPP implemented a risk and needs assessment instrument known as COMPAS (Correctional Offender Management Profiling for Alternative Sanctions; SCDPPP, 2012, p. 3). Preliminary assessments suggested an impact as fewer under supervised release were returned to prison (see Hester, 2016).

Era of Equilibrium

The changes embodied in the 2010 Crime Act reflected a new wave of sentencing reform laws across the country. Many states took measures to check the decades-long prison growth (see A. Austin, 2010; J. Austin, 2010). By 2010, for the first time since 1972, the number of prisoners in the United States did not increase but actually shrank by a small amount (Guerino et al., 2012; Mauer and Ghandnoosh, 2013). Tonry (2013, pp. 148, 150) has called the current era of sentencing a period of "equilibrium," characterized by a "nibbling at the ... edges" of the tremendous prison growth experienced in the get-tough era of mass incarceration. For years, critics have decried U.S. prison expansion and called for a substantial and deliberate reduction in the prison rate. So far, the new wave of reform does not appear to go that far.

First, much of the overall shift has been driven by reductions in a few states. For example, California reduced its number of prisoners by over 15,000 in just one year, from 2010 to 2011 (Petersilia and Cullen, 2014). The California reductions did not come as the result of legislative changes or even courtroom workgroup practices but instead were mandated by the U.S. Supreme Court (Petersilia and Cullen, 2014). Second, compared to the decades of expansion, the reductions have been modest. As Marc Mauer and Nazgol Ghandnoosh (2013) note, assuming the current rate of a less than 2 percent reduction per year, it would take 88 years to return the nation's prison rates to those in place in 1980, around the time the prison expansion began.

For South Carolina, there are preliminary suggestions that, for example, supervision revocations have declined since the 2010 Crime Act (Hester, 2016). However, a decline in South Carolina's prison rate began much earlier and was most likely based on budgetary crisis, and perhaps the operation of the DOC's good-time rules. As Figure 2.1 shows, the South Carolina prison rate grew steadily until it peaked at a rate of 556 in 100,000 in 2002. The prison rate then began a precipitous decline that continued through 2019. Between 2002 and 2010, South Carolina experienced a 12 percent decrease in its prison rate (from 556 to 490) without any substantial changes in sentencing laws.

The United States experienced two meaningful economic recessions between 2000 and 2015. While the financial collapse of 2008 had a much greater impact on the nation as a whole, the 2001 fiscal crisis significantly affected South Carolina, a state that had led the nation in per capita imprisonment for much of the 1980s and 1990s and that already had the most overburdened judiciary in the nation. State revenue dropped over 11 percent in 2002 alone, which was the sixth-largest decline of all states and three times the national median (Saltzman and Ulbrich, 2006). The South Carolina DOC was hit especially hard, experiencing a 21 percent reduction between 2000 and 2003, which the DOC describes as "the greatest percentage reduction of any correctional system in the country" (SCDOC, 2023, p. 19). There does not appear to be any direct evidence of official government calls to sentence fewer people to prison, and there were no significant remedial reforms—if anything the state was still well within the wake of the get-tough ethos, following TIS and three-strikes legislation. Yet

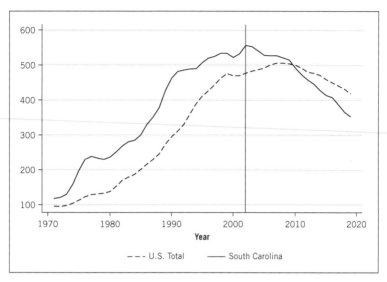

Figure 2.1 Imprisonment Rate per 100,000 (1971–2019) *Sources: Maguire and Flanagan (1990; covering 1971–1977); Carson (2020; covering 1978–2019).*

the imprisonment trends began to change, which must be a reflection of discretionary decision-making by court actors. While the change could simply be regression to the mean, court actor awareness of economic pressures fits within the theoretical expectations of the courts as communities perspective. In the face of this considerable economic pressure, courtroom decision-makers appear to have changed their sentencing practices to send fewer offenders to prison well before any formal changes that would come with the 2010 Crime Act.

This is quite an interesting empirical reality since the South Carolina incarceration rate reached its peak in the early 2000s (and the state had already stepped aside as the national leader in incarceration rates from the early 1990s) and has now dropped to about the middle of the pack in terms of state incarceration rates. This was the fourth-largest prison-rate drop among all of the states (Reitz et al., 2023), and it occurred with no major structural sentencing reforms during the period. The major trend downward began well before the omnibus 2010 legislation.

One explanation is that the exponential increase of incarceration rates stopped making sense at a point, and after a fourfold increase in imprisonment, court actors quietly eased off the gas pedal. The downturn of 2001 hit South Carolina's budget particularly hard—much harder than those in most states. Courtroom actors did not need to await formal legal changes in sentencing policy: the writing was on the wall. With budget cuts happening throughout all levels of state and local government, local court actors simply exercised their discretion to send fewer people to prison.

South Carolina stands as a bit of a sentencing policy enigma. No state exerted more effort over a longer period of time for guidelines only to come away empty handed. And yet, after leading as the most punitive state in the most punitive nation in the world, South Carolina found a way to ease itself of some of the glut of mass incarceration. The state was able to achieve sentencing reform without sentencing guidelines or the abolition of parole release discretion. There are, of course, other pressing concerns of the sentencing reform movement besides mass incarceration—including the mitigation of racial bias and geographic and interjudge disparities. But as we will see in the next chapters, South Carolina has fared remarkably well on those fronts too.

3

Sentencing without Guidelines

This chapter serves two primary purposes. The first part of the chapter presents the theoretical foundations relevant to understanding courts, sentencing, and racial disparities. These include the *focal concerns theory*, arguably the field's leading theory of individual-defendant sentencing decision-making, and the related *courts as communities* perspective and *inhabited institutions* perspective, which have a larger focus on local courts as social organizations with distinct local legal cultures. These (and related) theories provide a framework for thinking about how and why judges and other court actors assign the punishments they do. The frameworks also explain why racial disparities might emerge in punishment decisions and how individual judge characteristics and environmental factors like social, political, and economic characteristics affect punishment outcomes. The second part of the chapter provides empirical analysis of sentencing in South Carolina using the sentencing commission data supplemented by additional information collected on judge characteristics and attributes, as well as various county social, political, and economic factors. These results provide the rare look at sentencing in a nonguidelines state, offer some thought-provoking findings, and raise several questions that spawned a second phase of research (in the form of qualitative judge interviews) featured in subsequent chapters.

Defendant-Level Theories

Several related social-science-based theoretical ideas—uncertainty avoidance, causal attribution, and focal concerns—have been incorporated into the modern focal concerns theory (see Hester, 2012; Steffensmeier and Painter-Davis, 2018). These theories generally are rooted in the idea of symbolic interaction, a sociological tenet that holds that an actor's words and actions toward another entity are based on meanings the actor ascribes to the other person, event, situation, or thing (Blumer, 1969; Ulmer, 1997; Wooldredge, 2007). In the court context, symbolic interactionism suggests that judicial decision-making is a function of the meaning ascribed to an offender's characteristics, actions, and past behaviors—for example, the meaning a judge gives (even if subconsciously) to a "young person," a "Black man," a "violent offender," or a "repeat offender." More specifically, courtroom actors develop patterned responses to certain cues such as the seriousness of the offense, the presence of violence, and the defendant's criminal record, as well as extralegal characteristics like race, gender, and socioeconomic status (Albonetti, 1991; Steffensmeier, Ulmer, and Kramer, 1998).

One of the earliest applications of these ideas came with Celesta Albonetti's articulation of uncertainty avoidance and causal attribution at sentencing. Albonetti (1991) pointed to the bounded rationality that constrains sentencing decisions. Judges and workgroup members have limited information about the defendant and the crime, and they work in an overburdened space where efficiency concerns do not allow for time-consuming inquiries into most cases. In addition, workgroup members wish to avoid uncertainty, including on the question of whether a dangerous person might harm the community. Albonetti postulated that judicial decision-makers develop perceptual shorthands—basically stereotypes—and that these draw on racialized attributions (crime by minorities is seen as a reflection of intrinsic moral poverty or lack of character, while crime by whites is seen as explainable by extrinsic social or economic conditions) (Hester, 2012).

Perhaps more importantly, scholars have recognized that it is not only a shortage of time and information that leads to the development of stereotypes, typescripts, and imputations. When presented with an abundance of information, individuals tend to employ heuristics or shortcuts to simplify intellectual computation and facilitate a decision (Kahneman, 2011; Shah and Oppenheimer, 2008). Jeffrey Rachlinski and Andrew Wistrich (2017) reviewed a number of studies that found judges were strongly influenced by heuristics ranging from confirmation bias, numerical anchoring, race and gender influences, aversion to reversal, and election and retention pressures. According to Rachlinski and Wistrich (2017), judges are not more susceptible to heuristics and external influences than any other decision-makers, but they also are not immune to these influences: judges, too, are intuitive thinkers.

Darryl Steffensmeier and various colleagues articulated and advanced the focal concerns theory of sentencing (Steffensmeier, 1980; Steffensmeier and Demuth, 2001; Steffensmeier and Faulkner, 1978; Steffensmeier, Kramer, and Streifel, 1993; Steffensmeier and Terry, 1973; Steffensmeier, Ulmer, and Kramer, 1998).[1] According to focal concerns, there are three main considerations at sentencing: (1) judges are concerned with the moral blameworthiness of the defendant; (2) judges are concerned with the threat to public safety; and (3) judges may be influenced by a number of "practical constraints." Thus, the more heinous or aggravated the crime, the more harshly a defendant may be sentenced. The more a judge thinks a person is a threat to public safety, the more harshly they will be punished. And other practical constraints may result in a harsher or lighter sentence—for example, if local jail space is under stress, judges may become more likely to give probation in close cases. Steffensmeier and Noah Painter-Davis (2018, p. 195) offer these applications:

> Offense factors that shape perceptions of blame and risk include: the extent of harm that was caused, such as the amount of property damage or extent of victim injury; the vulnerability of the victim as indicated by victim characteristics, such as gender or age, that may shape the perceived severity of the crime in violent cases; the weight and type of illegal substance in drug cases; and the offender's role in the offense (e.g. instigator ver-

sus accomplice, dealer versus carrier). Prior criminal history, such as repeated involvement in crime or failed efforts to reform through more moderate interventions (parole, treatment programs), has a major impact on assessments of risk as well.

Steffensmeier and Painter-Davis (2018) also stress that focal concerns theory is integrative, not competitive vis-à-vis other theories. For example, a recent interest in the mechanisms of implicit bias has been incorporated into the script-building process of focal concerns (e.g., Lynch, 2019; Rachlinski et al., 2009; Tonry, 2010a).

Though it remains arguably the leading theory of sentencing, focal concerns theory has been criticized (see Lynch, 2019; Hartley et al., 2007; R. King and Light, 2019). Chief among the criticisms is that focal concerns tenants, while ubiquitously discussed, are almost never directly tested. Studies do not measure whether judges and prosecutors view Black defendants as more blameworthy or of higher risk. Instead, studies just find the presence or absence of disparities, and focal concerns theory serves as a framework for why disparities plausibly could exist. In addition, Mona Lynch (2019) observes that the theory suffers from both conceptual and operationalization problems. These include inadequate attention to the nature of institutionalized bias and insufficient connections between judicial bias and the psychological literature on attributions, bias, and cognitive processes. She expresses concern over the "virtual echo chamber" (p. 1168) produced by focal-concerns-based studies:

> Such studies are at their core descriptive, since as operationalized they measure the existence and extent of disparities. Yet, possibly due to the expectations of peer reviewed journals, many authors assert a more explanatory theoretical framework that hypothesizes why disparities may exist and how they are produced, with focal concerns as the dominant framework. (Lynch, 2019, p. 1162)

Similarly, Ryan King and Michael Light (2019) express concern over the theory's lack of specificity and its possible lack of falsifiability—"it generates ambiguous predictions that make it difficult to prove or disprove" (p. 411).

Regardless, focal concerns theory seems to serve the discipline well as an organizing perspective (e.g., R. King and Light, 2019, p. 412 ["focal concerns serve as a fine heuristic for thinking about what judges consider at sentencing, but the theory provides no clear guidance on when and where racial disparities should be most or least pronounced"]). While it is possible that direct racial animus exists, it seems likely that race has a more ephemeral influence, probably often working through implicit biases, and focal concerns provide plausible mechanisms of blame, risk, and practicalities through which those biases might manifest.

Over time, focal concerns theory has also integrated social organization concepts and has been fused with other broader theories relevant to sentencing—including social organization theory, the courts as communities perspective, and the framework of inhabited institutions. These broader theories incorporate institutional perspectives and county social, political, and economic context.

Organization-Level Theories

James Eisenstein and colleagues developed the courts as communities perspective as a theoretical framework for understanding the complex inner workings of court actors, their offices, and the political, social, and economic context in which each local court system operates (e.g., Eisenstein et al., 1988). This perspective draws on several important theoretical concepts, including the "courtroom workgroup" and "local legal culture." It emphasizes the courtroom workgroup, which is made up of the core courtroom actors assigned to a given case. The essential members are the prosecutor, judge, and defense attorney; in some jurisdictions other actors, such as probation officers, may also play a key role (Eisenstein and Jacob, 1977; Eisenstein et al., 1988). The way in which any particular workgroup functions varies depending on a variety of factors, including the attitudes and preferences of the workgroup members and the degree of stability, similarity, and familiarity among the members (Eisenstein et al., 1988; Metcalfe, 2016; Ulmer, 1997). Influence is exerted by the sponsoring organizations of the judge, prosecutor, and defense, and there is variation in the methods by which these organizations direct the individual actors in the workgroup, including the organizational structures, leadership styles, and historical relationships and power dynamics among the organizations. The interorganizational exchanges are further influenced by the emotional undercurrents within the court community, commonly shared workspaces, and the extent of informational grapevines (Flemming et al., 1992).

Beyond the workgroup members and their sponsoring organizations, environmental features of a local court community influence sentencing (Nardulli et al., 1988; Ulmer and Johnson, 2004). These include the social, economic, and political atmosphere of the place and linkages between the court community, the outside political and social community, and other influential local groups. Influences on county-level variation range from differences in the nature and flow of cases, the dominance of a large metropolis, and the expectations of the community and local elites to factors such as local jail and state prison capacity and media coverage of crime (Eisenstein et al., 1988; Nardulli et al., 1988). These influences capture notions of culture and sensibilities that shape punishment attitudes and outcomes (Garland, 2009, 2012).

Together, this rich bundle of factors operating at different levels works to shape the legal culture of a place. Legal culture can coalesce at different jurisdictional levels: county (or local) legal culture, state legal culture, and national legal culture (Eisenstein et al., 1988), though the overwhelming focus in the literature has been on local culture. A key component of local culture is the concept of "going rates," a term that refers to the standard penalties given to typical crimes and offender profiles or sentencing "templates" within a local jurisdiction (Ulmer and Johnson, 2004, p. 140). For example, although burglary may formally carry a wide punishment range, the local norms of a county may develop an informal expectation that a first-time nonviolent burglary offender receives two years' probation. In another county, characterized by more punitive sentiments, the going rate for a first-time burglar may be six months in jail. The communities perspective expects that different going rates will evolve on the basis of the particular legal culture of the locality and that these going rates will contribute to differences in sentencing outcomes (see also Sudnow, 1965). In short, the theory focuses on local county courts, their working norms, their organizational interrelationships, and the social and political climates they operate within. The thrust of the metaphor embodies a focus on interjurisdictional differences; as Eisenstein and his associates (1988, p. 56) put it, their objective was "to impart understanding of how courts differ, the *contours* of justice" (emphasis in original).

More recently, Jeff Ulmer (2019) has argued for courts to be considered under a framework of inhabited institutions. Ulmer is a leading scholar in both focal concerns and courts as communities literatures, and the inhabited institutions perspective incorporates elements of those traditions. The inhabited institutions perspective is a neoinstitutional theory that emphasizes the bottom-up cultural and interpretive processes that go into handling cases, the interdependencies of courtroom workgroup decision-making (especially between judge and prosecutor), and organizational mechanisms that lead to intercourt variations (Ulmer, 2019). Ulmer conceptualizes the court system as an institutional field with different courts (usually organized at the county level) comprising different organizations within that field. As Lynch (2019, p. 1165) observes, adopting the inhabited institutions means we "foreground the dynamic, contextual factors that create an operational milieu in which criminal case adjudication happens."

A central theme of the inhabited institutions perspective is that interorganizational variation creates localized adaptations. Thus, local courts will develop cultural characteristics that ultimately cause them to differ from one another—an idea very much in line with the courts as communities theoretical framework. Both inhabited institutions and courts as communities stress local legal culture differences in outcomes that would lead to county court differences. However, both frameworks also hold a place for individual actors, both as contributors to the culture and as direct influencers of outcomes.

Studies of court and county context support the idea that processing and sentencing norms vary substantially across locations within a jurisdiction (e.g., Bontrager et al., 2005; D'Alessio and Stolzenberg, 1997; Dixon, 1995; Johnson, 2006; Johnson et al., 2008; Kautt, 2002; Kramer and Ulmer, 2002; Ulmer and Johnson, 2004). However, as Brian Johnson (2006) has observed, it is difficult to concisely summarize the literature on how environmental characteristics influence sentencing outcomes. Some studies, for instance, find that factors like racial composition and socioeconomic conditions affect sentencing outcomes, while other studies do not (Johnson, 2006; Ulmer and Johnson, 2004). Though findings vary, the literature confirms the broad court communities proposition that location matters. As Ulmer and Johnson (2004, p. 140) assert, informal local norms appear to shape sentencing outcomes "at least as much as formal policies."

Empirical Findings in South Carolina

The remainder of this chapter presents empirical research on sentencing in South Carolina.[2] This begins with an analysis of defendant-level models of punishment and then proceeds to models that explore the influence of judge attributes and county contextual factors. The chapter concludes with a discussion of the key takeaways from this research.

The Methodological Appendix describes the data these results are derived from. As a brief overview, the data consists of 17,671 cases sentenced in the general jurisdiction trial courts of South Carolina in fiscal year 2001. The key outcome variables include a binary imprisonment indicator and a prison length measure for those incarcerated. The analyses discuss a number of independent variables, including controls for offense severity, defendant prior record, crime type, and demographic characteristics of age, race, and gender.

Defendant-Level Models

The empirical analysis begins with an exploration of the descriptive statistics. For the fiscal year of analysis, there were 17,671 offenders sentenced in the general jurisdiction courts of South Carolina. Table 3.1 provides descriptive statistics for the data. Even in the main trial court, most offenses were low- and midlevel felonies and serious misdemeanors. Over 60 percent of all cases were for the lowest two severity classifications—serious misdemeanor or Felony F, which carries a maximum five-year sentence. Only 8 percent of cases were in the four highest classifications of A, B, C, and exempt felonies.

Over a third of defendants (36.56 percent) had no prior criminal history. About a third were scored as minimal criminal history, with the remainder having a moderate to voluminous criminal record. The data also included an indicator of the number of charges the defendant was guilty of. The modal defendant had only one commitment offense (60.21 percent [not shown]), but because of the skew in those

TABLE 3.1. DESCRIPTIVE STATISTICS, SOUTH CAROLINA SENTENCING DATA

Variables	Mean	SD
Outcome Measures		
Incarcerated	.37	.48
Sentence Length in Months (1–470)	14.85	52.00
Predictors		
Offense Seriousness (1–8)	2.64	1.50
Criminal History (1–5)	2.14	1.19
Multiple Offense Score (1–12)	1.94	1.84
Trial Conviction	.01	.12
Mandatory Minimum	.05	.22
Offense Type Measures		
Homicide	.02	.12
Rape	.02	.13
Robbery	.03	.18
Aggravated Assault	.10	.30
Burglary	.12	.32
Drug Distribution	.17	.37
Drug Possession	.14	.35
Theft	.07	.26
Other	.21	.41
Fraud	.12	.32
Age Groups		
16–19	.10	.30
20–29	.39	.49
30–39	.30	.46
40–49	.16	.37
50 +	.05	.22
Race and Gender		
Black	.62	.49
Male	.83	.37

Note: $N = 17,671$

with more than one commitment score point, the mean commitment score was almost two. Criminal trials were exceedingly rare, with 98.54 percent of cases being resolved via guilty plea rather than a trial.

In terms of defendant characteristics, 83 percent were male, and the average (mean) age was 31. The 90th percentile for age [not shown] was at 45, and the 95th percentile was at age 50: the defendant population was much younger than the general population. This dataset was unfortunately not able to identify Hispanic ethnicity. The percentage of Black individuals was 62 percent, over twice the percentage of Black persons in the general population of South Carolina in 2000 (U.S. Census, 2001).

Sentencing Decisions

There are two main punishment outcomes traditionally analyzed in sentencing research: (1) whether a defendant was sentenced to prison and, (2) among that subset sent to prison, how long the period of incarceration was (here measured in months), operationalized as the minimum expected term to be served prior to parole eligibility. For these data, 6,611 (or 37.4 percent) were given an active incarceration sentence. Among those incarcerated, the average sentence was 39.6 months (about 3 years and 3 months), with a significant range. Figure 3.1 contains a schematic to illustrate these two key decisions. It is im-

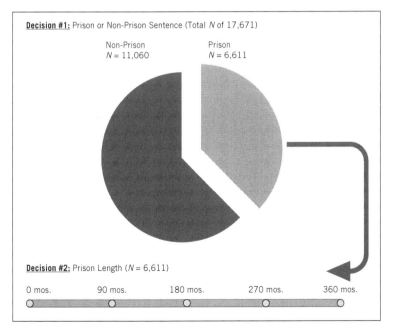

Figure 3.1 Schematic of Sample and Key Sentencing Decisions

portant to emphasize that these sentencing determinations take on two different data structure forms. The decision whether or not to imprison a defendant would be recorded as a binary entry (Prison: Yes/No; or 0, 1). Out of over 17,000 individuals who were sentenced, all have a Yes/No designation for prison, but only the subset of around 7,000 who received a prison sentence have data on the length of that prison term. This second outcome, prison length, is a continuous measure—a count of the number of months of the prison term, rather than a binary Yes/No measure.

For the prison length subset, Figure 3.2 provides a histogram, which graphically displays the distribution of prison sentence length, including nonprison terms (noted as 0 months). The figure is useful for illustrating the skew of the distribution with its long right tail, showing that, among those with a prison sentence, the vast majority were less than 100 months but that small numbers of longer sentences do appear, all the way up to 470 months. There are observable bumps in the high values, which correspond with preferred numbers like 120, 180, 240 (i.e., 10 years, 15 years, 20 years).

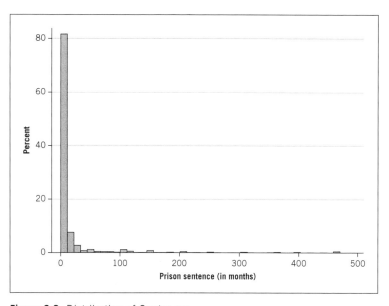

Figure 3.2 Distribution of Sentences

A detailed account of the statistical methods and analytic strategy used to examine this data, along with the description of the data, is provided in the Methodological Appendix. Briefly, the sections that follow present the results of regression analyses of the sentencing commission data. Regression is a statistical estimation technique that allows one to estimate the strength of the influence of a predictor variable of interest (like race) while controlling for other potentially important predictors of an outcome. For this project's analysis of sentencing in South Carolina, two different types of regression models form the basis for analyses, one for the prison in/out decision and another for the secondary prison sentence length decision, referenced in Figure 3.1.

In/Out Imprisonment Decision

The first analysis focuses on the decision of whether to sentence a person to some custodial sentence of incarceration or not (usually meaning a probation sentence instead). Since this is a binary decision, the statistical method for analyzing these prison decisions is known as a logistic regression. The results of the logistic regression predicting imprisonment are presented in Table 3.2.

The table reports several different statistics, including odds ratios, which are the traditional interpretive output for logistic regressions, standard errors, and the statistical significance indicators. For most readers, the average marginal effects (AMEs) will be the most interpretable statistic as they convey a percentage difference based on the predictor. Focusing on the AMEs, the table indicates that factors that have traditionally been considered "legal characteristics" increase the likelihood of an incarceration sentence, as one might expect. For predictors that are made up of multiple categories, like severity level and criminal history category, the AME coefficient applies to each one-unit increase in that measure. Thus, for each step up on the 1–8 scaled severity measure, the likelihood of incarceration goes up 8 percent. That means that a defendant with a severity offense category of 2 is 8 percent more likely to go to prison than a defendant with a category of 1 and that a defendant with a severity category of 3 is 16 percent more likely to go to prison than a defendant with a 1 (and a category 4 is 24 percent more likely and so forth). This impact is substantial when comparing low severity levels with high severity levels. Crimi-

TABLE 3.2. LOGISTIC REGRESSION MODEL OF THE IN/OUT DECISION

Variable	AME	OR	SE	p	
Offense Seriousness	.08	1.79	.05	.000	***
Criminal History	.13	2.76	.06	.000	***
Commitment Score	.04	1.41	.02	.000	***
Trial	.32	11.76	4.33	.000	***
Mandatory Minimum	.37	17.85	7.45	.000	***
Black	.06	1.54	.07	.000	***
Male	.07	1.69	.11	.000	***
Age Group (30–39 reference)					
16–19	−.03	0.79	.07	.005	**
20–29	.02	1.15	.06	.008	**
40–49	−.01	0.92	.06	.181	
50 +	−.03	0.81	.08	.037	*
Constant		0.00	.00	.000	***

Note: N = 17,670. Pseudo R^2 = .388. County fixed effects not shown.

nal history has a similar strong effect—a 13 percent increase in the likelihood of incarceration for each step from a criminal history category of none to minimal, moderate, extensive, and voluminous. Comparing the extremes, a defendant with a voluminous prior record would be 52 percent more likely to go to prison than one with no record, even if they were otherwise similar offenders convicted of the same current offense. Each additional conviction point brings a 4 percent increase in the likelihood of prison.

Having an offense with a mandatory minimum and choosing a trial rather than pleading guilty had the strongest effects, each increasing the likelihood of incarceration by over 30 percent. While this is expected for the mandatory designation, the mode of disposition finding is more complicated. The regression technique strives to provide an apples-to-apples comparison by controlling for everything the data allows us to control for. That means, in an examination of the impact of trial versus plea, other factors are accounted for to the extent possible, such as the type of offense, its severity, the defendant's prior record, and so forth. In other words, it may be that more serious cases go to trial because prosecutors are less likely to offer attractive plea deals or that defendants with extensive prior records are more likely to take a case to trial because it is unlikely they would be considered for probation. However, the regression analysis is already controlling for those factors; the observed trial effect exists above and beyond the correlations with those control variables. Thus the finding is interesting because there is no apparent legal reason a person should be punished more for exercising their constitutional right to a jury trial. And yet an offender who insists on a trial is 32 percent more likely to get a prison sentence than one who pleads guilty. Similar results have been found in research from other jurisdictions (e.g., Kramer and Ulmer, 2009), and scholars refer to this as a "trial penalty" (more on this later in this chapter).

Finally, the demographic characteristics have some impact on the likelihood of prison. Males are 7 percent more likely than women to be incarcerated, and Black defendants are 6 percent more likely than white defendants. Age exerts a modest influence, with those in their 20s 2 percent more likely to be incarcerated than those in their 30s (the comparison group) and with those younger than 20 and those 40 and older being a few percentage points less likely to be incarcerated.

One final note on the statistic labeled p on the table and accompanied by the statistical significance indicators of *, **, and ***. These indicate the construct of "statistical significance," which can be thought of as a measure of confidence in the veracity of the findings being reported (see Spiegelhalter, 2019). The statistic known as the p value measures the likelihood that the observed results are genuine and not a chance finding, with traditional p value thresholds being .05 (usually indicated by *), .01 (**), and .001 (***), the latter indicating the highest degree of confidence.

Sentence Length

The second major decision analyzed pertains to the subset of the 37 percent of individuals ($N = 6,611$) who were given a sentence of incarceration. For this analysis, the questions are how much time they will spend in prison and how the various factors of offense severity, prior record, age, race, gender, and so forth might influence the amount of prison time a person receives. Since South Carolina remains a parole state, it is possible that judges might factor in anticipated parole release into their sentence length decisions. This is especially so given the varying parole eligibility thresholds mentioned before—depending on classifications of violence and a TIS statute, parole eligibility can vary from a minimum time served of 25 percent to 33 percent or 85 percent. Obviously a 10-year sentence might mean something quite different if the parole eligibility is triggered at 25 percent or 85 percent of time served. To account for this likely influence on sentencing decisions, these models operationalize sentence length as the expected minimum sentence, accounting for parole eligibility classification. To analyze sentence length, scholars have commonly used a method known as ordinary least squares regression. The Methodological Appendix discusses some of the problems with this type of regression in this context and the reasons my colleague Dr. Todd Hartman and I adapted a modeling approach known as zero-truncated negative binomial hurdle regression to examine sentence length decisions (see also Hester and Hartman, 2017).[3] The results are provided in Table 3.3, where this time the AMEs provide estimates of the difference in number of months in prison.

Moving up the offense seriousness scale carries a strong association with prison time, about 21 months for each step on the scale. Surprisingly, criminal history has a muted effect on sentence length (only one additional month for each step up in prior record category), though it holds a strong connection to the previously examined in/out of prison decision. Trial versus plea again has a strong effect of over two ad-

TABLE 3.3. ZERO-TRUNCATED NEGATIVE BINOMIAL REGRESSION MODEL OF SENTENCE LENGTH

Variable	AME	Coef.	SE	p	
Criminal History	20.86	.49	.01	.000	***
Commitment Score	1.06	.03	.01	.002	**
Trial	3.33	.08	.00	.000	***
Mandatory Minimum	26.46	.62	.05	.000	***
Black	0.65	.02	.05	.739	
Male	2.70	.06	.02	.004	**
Age Group (30–39 reference)					
16–19	3.56	.08	.04	.016	*
20–29	2.01	.05	.04	.265	
40–49	−1.32	−.03	.02	.165	
50 +	1.36	.03	.03	.268	
Constant	7.99	.17	.05	.000	***

Note: $N = 6,610$. Pseudo $R^2 = .152$. County fixed effects not shown.

ditional years in prison (26 months) for going through with a jury trial rather than pleading guilty. Mandatory minimums had no relationship (though in a positive direction, the result was not statistically significant).

As to the demographic impacts, Black defendants received about 2.7 additional months in prison compared to similarly situated white defendants, and males received 3.6 months more than females. The age results were not statistically significant, with the exception of the 50-plus group, who received almost 8 more months than defendants in their 30s. (Note that this trend is in the opposite direction of the in/out effect, where older defendants were less likely to receive prison.) These results are discussed further at the end of this chapter, but first, we proceed with the judge and county empirical findings.

Judge- and County-Level Models

At the outset, it is worth noting that these empirical attempts are limited in their ability to probe the inner workings of court communities as inhabited institutions. This is precisely why Ulmer (2019) calls for mixed-method and qualitative approaches in his introduction of inhabited institutions. (Indeed, my research on South Carolina sentencing would eventually turn to qualitative interviews [see Chapters 4 and 5].) For now, I provide an overview of what could be investigated and what conclusions could be drawn with the quantitative data available.

Judges

The first set of analyses focused on potential judge-level influences. These are important for several reasons. First, although recent theorizing has refocused attention to the interactions between judges and prosecutors (e.g., Kim et al., 2015; Ulmer, 2019), many of the traditional concerns of fairness and sentencing emanate from the potential for unjustifiable differences in judges. Prosecutor identifiers are rarely available in sentencing datasets, but judge identifiers sometimes are, which has led to a line of research that examines the influence of judge-level characteristics and attributes on sentencing outcomes (e.g., Frazier and Bock, 1982; Johnson, 2006; Myers and Talarico, 1987; Spohn, 1990; Steffensmeier and Britt, 2001). The information about judges is often limited to what one can gather from biographical sketches, including things like prior legal experience, age, and gender.

For this research, I constructed a dataset of judicial attributes and investigated their influence using hierarchical linear models (see Methodological Appendix). Nine potential judge-level characteristics were initially collected for the 50 trial judges who were represented in the dataset. As elaborated in the appendix, these variables included the judge's race, gender, and age; the percentage of the legislature that was Republican in the year they were appointed to the bench; and the judge's prior prosecutorial experience, out-of-state law school, county rotation rate, and criminal caseload (selected on the basis of the relevant literature and available data). Since there were only 50 judges, the number of judge-level attributes had to be limited for methodological reasons related to statistical power. After bivariate correlations of the judge-level predictors and the sentencing outcomes were run, three variables emerged as appearing most correlated to the outcome and most theoretically relevant under the courts as communities perspective: judicial caseload, tenure on the bench, and prior prosecutorial experience.

The first analyses performed were unconditional models that provide an estimate of the level of variation in the outcomes of (1) the imprisonment decision and (2) the sentence length decision, attributable to the identity of the judge. Those full results are not shown here, but the findings were that about 7 percent of the variation in the imprisonment decision and just 2 percent in the sentence length decision were attributable to judge-level differences (see Hester, 2012). Given the lack of guidelines, this was somewhat surprising—the variation was less even than in guidelines jurisdictions (see Johnson, 2006).

Next, two separate multilevel models were estimated (one for in/out and one for length) with judge-level predictors included. The results (Table 3.4) are underwhelming in terms of the expectations that judge attributes might affect punishment outcomes. For both the in/out decision and length, there were practically no differences regardless of caseload, time on the bench, or prior prosecutorial experience. For the incarceration decision models, the odds ratios for caseload and tenure are nearly 1.00, meaning there is little practical substantive difference despite the statistically significant findings (indicated by * and **). For the sentence length model, none of the judge-level predictors was statistically significant, meaning we are unable to re-

TABLE 3.4. JUDGE-LEVEL EFFECTS ON SENTENCING OUTCOMES							
	Incarceration Decision				Sentence Length		
Variable	b	SE		OR	b	SE	
Intercept	−0.232	0.219		0.792	2.507	0.046	***
Judicial Caseload	−0.001	0.000	**	0.998	0.000	0.000	
Tenure	0.003	0.001	*	1.002	0.000	0.000	
Prior Prosecutorial Experience	−0.072	0.180		0.930	0.030	0.037	
N_1	17,516				6,569		
N_2	50						
Note: * $p \leq .05$; ** $p \leq .01$; *** $p \leq .001$							

ject the null hypothesis that judge-level predictors do not affect sentence length.

County

Next, a similar approach was taken with county-level analyses. The theoretical interest is in how the milieu of external influences on the court community can affect sentencing. These influences are complex and diffuse and surely vary from place to place. Scholars executing these sorts of quantitative studies tend to reduce to what data are readily available that might plausibly shed some light on social, economic, and political processes at the county level (Britt, 2000; Fearn, 2005; Ulmer and Johnson, 2004; Wang and Mears, 2010). Following this literature, I created a county-level dataset that included the percent voting Republican in the last presidential election, county criminal caseload, a concentrated disadvantage index, and a measure of the FBI Uniform Crime Reports index crime rate for each county. These were then analyzed with hierarchical linear models, similar to those used in the judge-level analyses.

As with the judge-level analyses, the county-level investigation began with unconditional models (not reported) to estimate the variance in outcomes attributable to the county level. Here, the county unit was responsible for only 2.4 percent and 2 percent of the variation in the incarceration and length decisions, respectively. Once again, the fully populated county-level findings were essentially null, as reported in Table 3.5. The only thing statistically significant was that a higher

TABLE 3.5. COUNTY-LEVEL MAIN EFFECTS ON SENTENCING OUTCOMES (INTERCEPTS AS OUTCOMES)

Variable	Incarceration Decision				Sentence Length		
	b	SE		OR	b	SE	
Intercept	0.250	0.320		1.280	2.570	0.120	***
Change in Concentrated Disadvantage	0.370	0.210	†	1.450	0.020	0.080	
Percentage Change in UCR Rates	0.190	0.270		1.210	−0.110	0.100	
Proportion Republican	−0.510	0.640		0.600	−0.070	0.230	
County Caseload	−0.030	0.010	*	0.970	0.000	0.000	
N_1	17,671				6,611		
N_2	46						

Note: † $p \leq .10$; * $p \leq .05$; *** $p \leq .001$

county caseload resulted in a slightly lower likelihood of the use of incarceration versus probation, but the size of the effect was not substantively significant at an odds ratio of .97 (a ratio of 1 means equal odds, so this was just slightly lower).

Discussion and Conclusion

The results of these empirical studies fill in some important gaps that existed in our knowledge of sentencing but also raise some additional questions. Of particular interest are findings related to the trial penalty and mandatory minimums, the different role that defendant criminal history had across the two outcomes of in/out and length, and the surprising levels of uniformity suggested by the judge and county analyses.

Overall Defendant-Level Findings

The main takeaway from the in/out statistical model results is that traditional legal characteristics are the driving force in the incarceration decision, as would be expected. Having a high-severity offense greatly increases the likelihood of incarceration rather than probation, as does an extensive prior record. Demographic characteristics had varying effects on incarceration, with Black defendants being 6 percent more likely to get prison, males 7 percent more likely, and age group affecting the likelihood by 2–3 percentage points. The sentence length model tells the same story for the most part. Legal characteristics account for most of the explanation. Again, a race disadvantage of 2.7 months' difference for Black defendants deserves further exploration.[4] The operations of prior record and the trial penalty are again notable.

Trial Penalty
The trial penalty is pronounced in both models, and the phenomenon is something scholars have written about extensively (e.g., Hester, 2019c; N. King et al., 2005; Ulmer and Bradley, 2006). Given the overwhelming predominance of plea bargaining in South Carolina, it is not surprising to find a robust trial effect. Most of the earlier research on trial penalties has reported odds ratios rather than average marginal effects. Those studies have found odds ratios of 2.7 in Pennsylvania for the in/out decision and a 57 percent increase in sentence length (Ulmer and Bradley, 2006); odds ratios of 2–3 in Kansas, Minnesota, Pennsylvania, and Washington (N. King et al., 2005); and odds ratios as high as 5–6 in Maryland. (For an overview of additional studies, see Kramer and Ulmer, 2009, pp. 140–141.) Here, for the in/out decision the odds ratio in South Carolina is 11.76—quite pronounced by comparison.

As discussed in Hester (2019c), since a jury trial is a constitutional right, questions arise as to why availing oneself of a jury trial carries such a severe penalty. There are several potential explanations. Trial penalties may reflect the organizational efficiency concerns of prosecutors, judges, and defense attorneys (Kramer and Ulmer, 2009; see also Dixon, 1995). Trials consume much more time and resources than pleas. In other U.S. jurisdictions, the trial rate is around 5 percent; for these South Carolina data, it is less than 2 percent. From a behavioral economics standpoint, system actors must incentivize guilty pleas to keep up with unceasing caseload demands.

Conceptually, we lack an anchoring point for defining the ideal sentence: It is unclear whether those who go to trial are simply getting what they deserve and those who plead guilty are getting rewarded for a sentence more lenient than they deserve because of their cooperation or whether the 98 percent of defendants who plead guilty are getting what they deserve and the 2 percent who insist on a trial are getting penalized for their insistence on taking up the court's time. Aside from the pure economy of it all, judges may feel that defendants who are remorseful and accept responsibility for their actions deserve mercy (in line with the discount idea discussed earlier in this chapter). John Kramer and Ulmer (2009, p. 100) present evidence from qualitative interviews of Pennsylvania judges, such as one who said: "People who plead guilty always argue that remorse is a mitigating factor, and one cannot deny that. They are saying, 'I'm sorry, I did it.' I consider that a mitigating factor. . . . You could look at it as a penalty but there is no other way of doing it. You have to give people credit for pleading guilty and expressing remorse."

As yet another possible contributor to trial penalty findings, trials may bring out all of the gory details of a crime that are otherwise kept under cover in a guilty plea. Kramer and Ulmer (2009) call this the bad facts thesis (see also Brereton and Casper, 1981). As explored in Hester (2019c), under this view, hearing eyewitness accounts, testimony about victimization, and narratives from the victims may leave a strong emotional impression that leads the judge to pursue the upper ends of punishment. It may be one thing to hear a prosecutor's cold recitation of the facts that "the defendant did commit a burglary on or around such-and-such a date, having broken and entered a given residence at nighttime, and stolen personal property of the homeowner valued at x dollars." It may be quite another to hear the homeowner's tearful account of fear and distress upon finding her home burglarized, her things rifled through, valued items taken and never recovered, and her persistent fear of having her home intruded into again. If the emotive impact of these details drew out harsher punishment, it would be based on a more informed appreciation of the case itself rather than an attempt to penalize the individual for exercising their constitutional right. Nevertheless, the differential between trial and plea outcomes seems quite striking considering that the regression analyses are comparing otherwise similar cases with the primary difference being the exercise of a constitutional right.

Mandatory Minimums

One other observation about these results relates to the mandatory minimum findings. Mandatories are notorious sentencing "reform" impositions (Tonry, 1992, 2006). Legislatures impose their will, often in a politicized, get-tough context, by expressing that for certain crimes (usually drug and gun related) no person or circumstance would merit a probation sentence—everyone must do a predetermined number of years in prison. What is intriguing about the findings here is that mandatories, by definition, impose a strong prediction for the in/out decision. However, judges would be free to impose additional time above and beyond the mandatory minimum, up to whatever the statutory maximum is for the offense. If the legislature had identified for a mandatory minimum designation a class of offenses that touched on a heightened blameworthiness (as sexual assault might) or posed a particular threat to public safety, we might expect to see that reflected in the sentence lengths, which remain within the discretion of the court actors. If a drug crime carries a mandatory one-year sentence, that defendant must receive at least a one-year sentence, but they could receive well over a year. These findings indicate that mandatory offense defendants do not receive longer prison terms, suggesting that court actors do not necessarily see these offenses as particularly bad and that the prison terms imposed are already longer that what court actors—the experts with boots on the ground—would impose.

Criminal History
The prior record findings here are intriguing, and significant given that this is one of the only available datasets of sentencing in a state without sentencing guidelines. Almost all sentencing research in the past 30 years has come from sentencing guidelines states. Sentencing guidelines usually are structured around a two-dimensional grid or matrix (see Table 6.1 in Chapter 6). By design, the guidelines impose increasing punishment both vertically (more serious current offense) and horizontally (more extensive prior record). Later, in Chapter 5, this book explores the 1960s and 1970s sentencing guidelines formation studies and documents in an effort to uncover exactly how these two-way matrices came to be. Empirical studies show that most people generally agree with a hierarchy of offense seriousness—that murder and rape are among the worst crimes and should be punished most harshly, that petty theft and simple possession of drugs are among the least egregious crimes and should be punished less harshly, and so forth. However, the role and relevance of prior record is less clear and agreed upon (see Hester, Roberts, et al., 2018).

Certainly, prior record has some significance in sentencing, but it is not obvious that it would lead the average person, or judge, to a mathematically formulated relationship to punishment as is found in sentencing guidelines. The traditional legal-philosophical justifications for punishment are retribution and consequentialism (or utilitarianism). Retribution is backward looking; it seeks to assess blameworthiness and to apportion an appropriate proportional negative consequence onto the perpetrator. Importantly, criminal law punishes criminal acts, not status or moral state separate from an illegal act (*Robinson v. California*, 1962). It may be a crime to use illicit drugs, but it is not a crime to be a drug addict, and likewise it is not a crime to be a person who has committed prior crimes—it is only a crime when a new offense is committed. Thus, even if a lay person were to disapprove of a convicted burglar or think less of them for their past, the law cannot punish them (again) for the status of a prior convict. Consequently, for a judge to punish a defendant more on account of their prior record under a purely retributive rationale, the judge would have to conclude that the defendant is more blameworthy *for the current offense of conviction* than a similarly situated defendant guilty of the same crime but without a prior record. In Hegel's treatment of retribution, he speaks of the crime being "cancelled" upon service of the punishment (still a popular notion associated with the phrase "he paid his debt to society") (see Tonry, 2010b, p. 49). If service of the punishment cancels the crime, then how can it be uncanceled? Commission of a new crime simply creates a new debt to be paid. Hester, Frase, Roberts, and Mitchell (2018) provide an extended survey of the unsatisfying attempts of legal scholars and philosophers to articulate a convincing theory of why a defendant with a prior record should be punished more harshly under a retributive rationale. Probably the most convincing theory is Andreas von Hirsch's (2010) progressive loss of mitigation theory. He suggests that first or early-career offenders are given less than what they deserve—they are given mitigated sentences and second chances. However, after two, three, or some other number of offenses, they no longer receive mitigation and instead begin to receive the just penalty for the crime. Notice, however, that punishment premiums under this account would not continue to grow with each prior offense as they do in guidelines systems.

The second school of punishment justification is consequentialism (or utilitarianism) and includes theories of deterrence, incapacitation, and rehabilitation. Under these theories, the only purpose of imposing punishment is to reduce the causes or consequences of future crime. Thus, a more severe sentence might be appropriate for a defendant with a prior record if (1) that prior record made them more likely to reoffend or cause more damage in the future and (2) the more severe punishment would thereby reduce the likelihood or intensity of that future wrongdoing. Consequentialism could provide a strong basis for prior record enhancements: It is well known that past behavior predicts future behavior. However, there are two problems. First, it needs to be demonstrated that the increased punishment for a prior record corresponds to the increased risk based on that prior record. For example, if a punishment system added a 25 percent premium in punishment for every serious prior felony conviction, it should be true that each serious prior was associated with some increase in the likelihood of reoffending; otherwise, the additional punishment is gratuitous. In an article published in the *American Journal of Criminal Justice*, I examined this question using the Pennsylvania Sentencing Guideline's Prior Record Score (PRS) (Hester, 2019a). Using a technique known as survival analysis (Cox proportional hazards regression), I found that some of the prior record categories in fact did not correspond with an increased risk of recidivism. Further, almost all the power of the PRS's ability to predict future recidivism was found in the simple binary distinction of whether a person had no prior record or any prior record. Thus, the intricate counting and scoring scheme and the increasing levels of punishment given to individuals with higher scores, as implemented, were not fully justifiable on consequentialist grounds.

Even if a jurisdiction's scoring scheme aligned with an increased risk of recidivism, there is a second problem. Consequentialism requires that the punishment imposed be tailored to reduce the causes or consequences of crime. As elaborated by Hester, Frase, Roberts, and Mitchell (2018), there is unfortunately little reason based on current research to believe that the additional punishment an offender receives in the form of a prior record premium will rehabilitate them, deter them, or deter others. It will, by definition, incapacitate them for that exact amount of time, but incapacitation has not traditionally been viewed as a tool appropriate for the short-term targeting of nonviolent offenders. Pursuant to consequentialism, the crime avoidance costs must outweigh the punishment imposition costs, which will rarely be true of incapacitation for nonviolent crimes (Hester, Frase, Roberts, and Mitchell, 2018; Hester, Frase, Laskorunsky, and Mitchell, 2019).

Despite these potentially serious limitations, guidelines jurisdictions impose substantial sentence enhancements based on prior record. A study by Frase and colleagues (2015) found that guidelines impose an average of around a 600 percent increase in sentence comparing offenders with no prior records to those in the highest guideline criminal history category. In some jurisdictions, the increase was over 1,000 percent. Chapter 5 reports on a historical analysis that attempts to uncover the origins of these formulas and reports evidence that these criminal history premiums were not empirically based in the way early adopters might have assumed. For now, the point is that the findings from South Carolina offer a stark and important contrast to how judges might treat prior record when not under guidelines constraints. The muted importance of prior record for sentence length in South Carolina, coupled with the unintended collateral consequences of racial disparities and overuse of prison, plus the questions about punishment justifications for prior record enhancements, might lead guidelines jurisdictions to rethink their criminal history polices.

Judge and County Findings

There are ample reasons in the theoretical literature to expect meaningful judge- and county-level influences on sentencing, as suggested by a variety of theoretical perspectives related to judicial attitudes and preferences and to differences in local court communities. Admittedly, the empirical findings from earlier studies on these matters are mixed and inconclusive in many respects, but under any account, the results from South Carolina are intriguing. Most notable are: (1) the much smaller levels of variation attributable to judges (for the length decision) and county (for both the binary incarceration and sentence length decision) and (2) the nearly total null findings for the influence of caseload, tenure, and prosecutorial experience for the judge models and the concentrated disadvantage, crime rates, political makeup, and county caseload for the county models. The county-level findings were especially perplexing given prior research where a hallmark of the theory is that sentencing differences will exist in local legal cultures.

Given that most recent sentencing research has been in guidelines states and that most of it found evidence of racial disparities (at least for the incarceration decision) and judge and county variation, how much more would be present in South Carolina, a nonguidelines state in the Deep South, at one time the leader in the competitive field of mass incarceration, and a state with an entrenched history of racial issues from slavery and its role in the Civil War right up to the current era? (Recall that this dataset is from 2000–2001. The Confederate flag flew from the dome of the South Carolina Statehouse until July 1, 2000, when it was moved a few feet away to a prominently placed monument directly in front of the Statehouse. It remained there until it was finally removed in 2015 in the aftermath of the racially motivated shooting massacre that killed nine people at Emanual African Methodist Episcopal Church in Charleston, South Carolina.)

A New Phase of Research

These questions led me to a new phase of research. Because the courts as communities perspective is focused on explaining variation, the potential for more uniform statewide culture and norms has been overlooked. Yet the idea that variation among court communities exists along a continuum is implicit in the theory: At one extreme would be a greatly diffuse and independent set of county courts characterized by stark differences in cultures, norms, and outcomes. At the other extreme would be communities characterized by remarkable uniformity. County location should be highly salient to outcomes where state legal culture casts negligible influence and other community characteristics work to maximize the development of divergent local norms. But if instead state legal culture were strong and pervasive enough, it would work to normalize outcomes and practices at the expense of local variation.

This possibility of stronger statewide culture is suggested on several occasions in the courts as communities literature. For instance, Peter Nardulli, James Eisenstein, and Roy Flemming (1988, p. 30) point to environmental factors that include socioeconomic structure, political makeup, and "a structural-legal domain embodying relevant laws, codes, and rules, as well as facilities." Environmental factors can have both a county and a state dimension. One example, referred to throughout the communities texts, is the constraining effect of limited state prison capacity. Where a state is experiencing a severely overburdened prison system, space limitations might constrain workgroups across counties to temporarily reserve incarceration for only the most serious offenders. In less austere times, more options may be presented, and thus greater room for variation may emerge.

Other aspects of the communities theory can be extrapolated to account for a statewide culture in ways that were not necessarily anticipated by Eisenstein and colleagues. For instance, Nardulli, Eisenstein, and Flemming (1988, p. 41) recognize that court system infrastructure variants are "important to note because they have an important impact upon the terrain in a court community." One example is the infrastructure characteristic of judicial calendaring. In some places an individual calendaring system assigns a case to the same judge for the duration of the judicial process, while other counties use a master calendaring system. In the master calendaring system, different judges handle different aspects of the case (indictment, pretrial motions, disposition, sentencing, etc.). Master calendaring opens up an opportunity for judge shopping, when, for example, an attorney is able to persuade a court administrator to route a case into a particular judge's courtroom or when an attorney delays a case set for sentencing so that case may be heard by a more favorable judge at a later date (Eisenstein et al., 1988; Ulmer, 1997). In contrast, Ulmer (1997, p. 83) found that the individual calendaring systems used in two of the counties he studied made judge shopping "nearly impossible."

In South Carolina, a variant of master calendaring is imposed centrally on all counties. Rotation requires judges to preside in workgroups throughout the state and means that a local court receives many different judges in the course of the year. Nardulli, Eisenstein, and Flemming (1988, p. 164–165) speculate in passing that "diffusion of innovations, structures, and practices brought about by statewide meetings, publications, and grapevines may lead to structures that one may not otherwise expect to find." Eisenstein, Flemming, and Nardulli (1988, p. 50–51) make a similar observation about the "indirect effects from the general context of the state": "Both state political culture and interaction among judges, prosecutors, and others in state meetings produce some 'norming effects' on things like severity of sentences and technologies used. . . . Thus, states exhibit a state legal culture that produces differences on matters not encompassed by the national legal culture." By producing a web of cross-jurisdictional networks and facilitating the sharing of ideas, rotation could lead to the cross-pollination of perspectives and practices and a resulting norming effect from these extensive interactions.

Eisenstein and associates found only weak state legal culture influences in their foundational work. Subsequently, studies have tended to disregard state legal culture, focusing instead on differences among local courts, the heart of the theory. Accordingly, the theoretical mechanisms that might lead to greater uniformity among court communities have remained underdeveloped. In fact virtually no progress has been made on exploring variations in the degree of local legal culture divergence, though geographic uniformity—ensuring that like cases are treated alike throughout a state—appears to be an important issue for scholars and policymakers.

To probe deeper into the findings on uniformity and the use of prior record, I began a new phase of research focused on conducting qualitative interviews with the state's trial judges, which are the focus of the remaining chapters.

4

Judicial Rotation as Centripetal Force

The inspection of the South Carolina sentencing data described in Chapter 3 raised as many questions as it provided answers about punishment practices in the state. Though the state is a Deep South stronghold with an abundance of racial baggage, the data uncovered mixed race effects in punishment outcomes. Just as surprising, for a nonguidelines state in which judges retained vast discretion over sentencing decisions, the outcomes in South Carolina appeared to be remarkably uniform from judge to judge and county to county. To obtain deeper and richer insights into these sentencing practices and outcomes, the project turned to a different method of inquiry: qualitative interviews of the state's trial judges. The findings from these interviews are discussed in this chapter. The interview findings highlight the pervasive influence of one obscure vestige of the state's judicial structure: the retained practice of having judges ride circuit, or routinely travel to preside over court in counties throughout the state.

Social scientists refer to the types of analyses presented in Chapter 3 as quantitative studies—generally meaning that the researcher is using a sufficiently large data source (in our case, there were over 17,000 sentencing outcomes in the dataset, with dozens of pieces of information about each of those 17,000 observations) to generate statistical tests about relationships in the data. Having thousands of cases making up the full universe of observations has great benefits for examining relationships of interest, such as for answering a question like, What are the differences in sentences given to Black and white individuals for a similar offense? Yet quantitative data can only tell us so much. Crunching data might be able to tell us whether or not Black defendants get sentenced more severely, but data crunching cannot necessarily tell us why. Big data also cannot provide much insight into why racial disparities seemed modest in South Carolina or why sentencing seemed relatively uniform from county to county despite the absence of unifying guidelines. For deeper explanations, social scientists turn to qualitative studies or ethnographies as a way to generate deeper and richer explanations for observed phenomena (e.g., van Cleve, 2016). Qualitative studies such as the interviews of 13 judges presented in this chapter are aimed at generating deeper potential explanations.

The research reported in this chapter was undertaken to shed light on these unexpected findings. South Carolina continues to employ the practice of judicial rotation, in which all judges travel from county to county to hold court. The results presented in this chapter suggest that the continued practice of circuit rotation by the trial judges serves as a centripetal unifying force of sentencing culture, homogenizing what might otherwise be a much more varied collection of county- and judge-specific sentencing norms. Judicial rotation allows defendants to judge shop by waiting to enter a guilty plea when a lenient or favorable judge comes to town. This phenomenon gives rise to the "plea judge," an informal title used to refer to lenient judges who sentence a disproportionately large number of defendants because of the judge shopping. Throughout the interviews, the continuum of more to less punitiveness played a prominent role and was most readily identified by the two outcomes frequently analyzed in criminological sentencing research: how often a judge sentenced offenders to prison—the in/out decision—and the length of prison stay imposed on those who were thus sentenced—the length decision.

Judge Interviews

The appendix provides a more technical account of the qualitative interview methodology, but some general information is useful for all readers here. South Carolina has one of the highest judge-to-caseload ratios in the country, and in the time frame for the sentencing commission data, there were only about 50 full-time general jurisdiction trial judges serving the state's population of 4 million. At that time there was very little diversity on the bench (though that has changed over time). The goal was to identify enough of these judges to provide for a "full and complete description" (Becker, 1998) that would "saturate" the subject questions and render generalizable findings (Creswell, 2014). On average, the 50 judges held court in 12 different counties in 2001; thus adequate coverage was almost guaranteed because of the extensiveness of rotation. The 13 judges ultimately interviewed held residency in 10 of the 16 circuits (two were "at large," and two were residents in the same county) and sentenced offenders in all but 4 of the state's 46 counties during 2001. Thus, on the particular question of the likely influence of judicial rotation, the judges provided considerable geographical coverage and would all be well suited to provide an informed perspective on county differences.

I did however want to ensure that I leveraged variation among the judges. Most significantly, I wanted to speak with judges at different points along the continuum of punitiveness. Presumably there are meaningful differences in punishment preferences among judges, but attributes like race, gender, and age appear to be poor proxies for these attitudes and preferences.[1] Using the sentencing data referenced in Chapters 3 and 4, I constructed two measures of punitiveness: the percentage of offenders incarcerated and the average prison sentence length for those sent to prison. To supplement the punitiveness measures, I considered the judges' judicial caseloads for the year. And although the results on judge attributes have been mixed, they remain theoretically relevant, so I factored in gender,[2] age, and time on the bench as secondary considerations for choosing among judges who fell on similar places along the punitiveness continuum. The final sample of 13 represents considerable geographic coverage of the state and provides representation along the potentially relevant characteristics of punitiveness, caseload, gender, age, and tenure.

Interview Findings

The interview data revealed that judicial rotation has a defining influence on creating a more statewide legal culture. The resulting pull toward uniformity occurs through two primary mechanisms: (1) judge shopping and (2) the cross-pollination of ideas and practices.

Circuit Rotation and Plea Judges

The most enlightening theme to emerge from the interviews was the defining influence of the judges traveling through the different counties. Judicial rotation, the practice of a judge holding court in multiple counties throughout the year, acts as a centripetal legal cultural force that pulls together would-be disparate, localized practices into a more uniform set of statewide norms. Traveling engenders an openly embraced practice of judge shopping and plea routing, the result of an extreme and unique form of statewide master calendaring. A judge's reputation is quickly established and spreads throughout the state, and judges readily self-identified as being "harsh," "stringent," or "tough," on the one hand, or "lenient" or a "plea judge," on the other hand. The informal term "plea judge" is routinely used to refer to lenient judges who sentence a larger proportion of the state's criminal cases because of judge shopping.

Rotation allows defendants to avoid tough judges by waiting for a plea judge to come to town. Several judges gave accounts of tough "hanging judges" who would travel to a circuit for a week of court and by Tuesday would have no one pleading guilty in front of them: criminal court business would essentially shut down for the week. As Judge Hall[3] explained, "The lawyers know if there's a harsh judge they can just not plead and wait for a plea judge, and if the solicitor wants to put the case on the trial docket they can do that, but chances are before the case comes up another judge will come to town." Accordingly, said the same judge, "sentencing ends up being on the shoulders of judges whose sentences are the lightest"—the plea judges. Judge Andrews gave a more pointed account: "One month Judge Softy is coming to town, so there's a waiting list for Judge Softy. Everybody games the system. The attorneys say, 'Oh, I'm gonna be on vacation this week, but I'll be back the week Judge Softy is here.'" In contrast, when a plea judge is holding court, business is brisk and defendants readily enter pleas.

Even prosecutors and the more punitive judges appreciate and rely on the efficiency role served by the plea judges. As Judge Hall again explained, "When solicitors look at their dockets, they want to move cases. They might want an outcome in a particular case, but they can also step back and look at their entire caseload, and they want cases to move. So they want these [plea] judges too." Judge Darnell, a self-proclaimed "stringent" judge, spoke favorably of having plea judges rotate into his home circuit because it "helps clear out the docket, and that's good."

In fact, because prosecutors have control of the docket, they can assign the harsher judges to trials and have plea judges take pleas for an entire week of criminal court, thereby ensuring a steady disposition of cases. In this way, plea judges contribute to greater uniformity in sentencing throughout the state. Defense attorneys can hold out for a plea judge, and when one comes to town, defendants line up to plead guilty. Because defendants can openly judge shop, the more lenient plea judge standards of sentencing become the foundation for going rates (or standard sentences for typical crimes).

This does not mean that a few plea judges hold prosecutors hostage by continually lowering the sentencing floors. Prosecutors have tremendous power and discretion—over filing charges, bargaining, calling cases for trial, and assigning a judge to preside over pleas or trials for a given week. Prosecutors are also able to game the system by holding out the opportunity to be sentenced by a plea judge as a carrot and using the threat to call the case for trial in front of a hanging judge as a stick. The phenomenon of the plea judge and the concomitant sentencing norms appear to represent the organic development of sentences that are acceptable to both prosecutors and defense attorneys, optimal going rates that facilitate the pleading out of over 98 percent of felony offenders in an acutely overburdened criminal justice system.

Judge shopping and plea routing do not only affect sentencing by getting more cases pleaded in front of the most lenient judges; some non-plea judges also adjust their sentencing preferences in light of the reality of shopping for plea judges. These pragmatic sentencers soften their preferences or accept more negotiated or recommended sentences to continue to hear cases and keep the docket moving. Judge Darnell, who described his reputation as "I don't want to say severe, but... severe," stated, "Straight-up pleas don't happen. I take negotiated or recommended sentences in 80 or 90 percent of cases. Some judges won't, but I'm pragmatic about it. We need to move cases." Judge Frank similarly expounded,

> It's necessary to take recommendations within a range everybody can live with. There are a few judges who won't take recommendations or negotiations—these hanging judges or Maximum Bobs or what have you. But defendants won't plead before them unless they have some idea of what the sentence will be. And the solicitors don't want it either because plea courts will shut down. By Tuesday nobody's pleading. So judges who hear pleas are all on the same page as far as acceptable ranges.

For judges like this, defendants are reluctant to plead straight up with no recommendation, and prosecutors, ever mindful of the need to move cases, accommodate through recommendations acceptable to the defense. Although some judges stated that a recommendation was made in at least a majority of cases, Judge Matthews, a plea judge, indicated that there were no recommendations or negotiated sentences in at least 90 percent of his cases because "they [the attorneys] know me and know what to expect." Apparently, interjudge differences in the mode of plea accepted (straight, recommended, or negotiated) were in part a product of whether the attorneys felt the need for assurances a sentence would comply with the going-rate norms of the plea judges.[4]

Some of the harsher judges hold firm to their punitive practices and are therefore more likely to be assigned to trials rather than plea weeks or to simply sentence fewer cases during plea weeks. Judge Iredell, a harsh sentencer (who also refused to accept negotiated pleas), reflectively wondered whether his "old-school" approach was the right one. But after talking it through, he assured himself, "The legislature elected me to impose the sentence, not the solicitor or defense attorney. Bottom line is, that is up to me. I guess for that reason I ended up being a trial judge in a lot of cases." He was then asked, "Why? Solicitors would assign you to a trial and let more lenient judges take plea weeks?" He answered, "I guess, a lot of times."

Other "hanging judges" appeared to simply be marginalized by boredom when defendants refused to plead in front of them. At first I thought the stories of the hanging judge sitting around in an empty courtroom were apocryphal, but over the course of the interviews, several judges gave firsthand accounts of this phenomenon. Judge Eliot recounted, "You'll go to another jurisdiction, and you'll only be there a week—and it's frustrating, and it may even be unethical—but the lawyers will shut down on you." Judge Coleman volunteered, "This one circuit told me all the cases would be negotiated pleas because they didn't like my sentences. So I said we might as well just stop now then." Judge Andrews also conveyed experiences of court weeks in which no one would plead in front of him, and the concern was great enough that Judge Hall noted he was more deferential to recommendations when out of his home district because "if you don't play ball, they'll shut down on you." Thus, defendants and defense counsel "shutting down" on an inflexible judge appeared to be a real possibility.

One of the central findings from the interviews was the account of the less severe plea judges sentencing more offenders because of the opportunity to judge shop created by judicial rotation. I used the South Carolina sentencing data to quantitatively examine that proposition. Panels A and B of Figure 4.1 provide empirical corroboration of the judges' accounts of the relationship between leniency and the number of offenders sentenced. Panel A shows a scatter plot of the percentage of offenders incarcerated (the in/out decision) by the total number of offenders sentenced for each of the 50 judges represented in the data. Panel B provides the same for the average prison sentence imposed (in months) by the number of offenders sentenced. Both figures also include a predicted or fitted values line, which was derived by regressing the number of offenders sentenced on the outcome measure. The down-sloping fitted values line in each figure confirms the interview accounts of plea judges—as punitiveness decreases, the number of offenders sentenced increases.[5]

Table 4.1 is also instructive. It lists each judge interviewed and provides their rank according to their incarceration percentage, average months of prison imposed, and number of offenders sentenced. Judges Andrews and Iredell were in the top three for the punitiveness measures and were the top two in fewest offenders sentenced. At the other extreme, Judges Keates, Matthews, and Hall were the bottom three

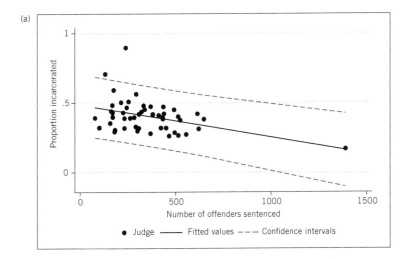

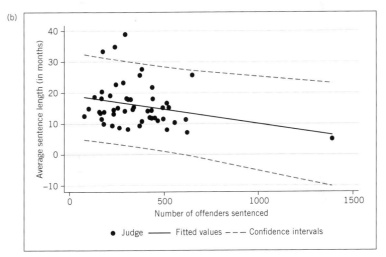

Figure 4.1 Relationship between Punitiveness and Number of Offenders Sentenced. Panel A: In/Out Punitiveness. Panel B: Length of Time Punitiveness (*Notes: The y axis represents the punitiveness measure [for Panel A, the raw percentage of offenders imprisoned; for Panel B, the mean expected minimum prison length (in months) of offenders imprisoned by the judge]; the x axis indicates the number of offenders sentenced by that judge for the year. The figures were derived by conducting regression in which the number of offenders sentenced was used to predict the punishment outcome.*)

TABLE 4.1. JUDGE RANK BY PUNITIVENESS AND OFFENDERS SENTENCED; REPRESENTATIVE STATEMENTS OF SENTENCING PHILOSOPHY

Judge Pseudonym	In/Out Rank	Prison Length Rank	Offenders Sentenced Rank	Representative Statements of Sentencing Philosophy and Punitiveness
Andrews	1	1	2	"I'm probably considered . . . harsh is probably too strong a word, but I guess harsh"; claimed to be lenient on low-level drug offenses
Iredell	2	3	1	Self-described as "tough"; refused to accept negotiated pleas; assumed he heard more trials as a result
Darnell	3	2	7	Self-described as "severe"; 80–90% of sentences negotiated or recommended: "Some judges won't [take negotiated pleas], but I'm pragmatic about it. We need them to move cases"; mentioned offender age and influence of victims and their families
Garland	4	5	6	Did not mention extralegal characteristics; often takes quasi recommendations from prosecution in the form of "we're not opposed to a sentence of . . ."
Frank	5	4	5	Influenced by offender age, education, employment, and family and community support; often preferred a fine to probation for certain low-level offenses
Jenkins	6	7	8	Mentioned defendants' "support system"; takes negotiated or recommended plea "probably one-third of the time"; sees role of traveling judge as maintaining some uniformity in outcomes across counties
Coleman	7	6	9	Stated, "Sentencing is the hardest part about being a judge"; "I'm not a big fan of LWOP—it's like a sledgehammer"
Lyndon	8	9	10	Estimated he takes recommended pleas in 70% of cases, negotiated sentences in 5%, and straight pleas 25% of the time; did not mention any extralegal characteristics
Eliot	9	8	3	Discussed the importance of job, social stability, who the offender lives with, work history, and attitude; stressed the need for rehabilitation and restitution; wished for more funding for halfway houses

TABLE 4.1. JUDGE RANK BY PUNITIVENESS AND OFFENDERS SENTENCED; REPRESENTATIVE STATEMENTS OF SENTENCING PHILOSOPHY (*continued*)

Judge Pseudonym	In/Out Rank	Prison Length Rank	Offenders Sentenced Rank	Representative Statements of Sentencing Philosophy and Punitiveness
Bates	10	10	4	Will not accept negotiated pleas but looks to recommendations from prosecution and defense; conscious of prison and jail overcrowding; did not mention extralegal characteristics
Keates	11	12	12	"You try to consider everything made known to you"; straight-up pleas in 90% of cases: "They know me and what to expect"
Matthews	12	11	11	Self-described as "lenient unless it's aggravated or something"; stressed importance of keeping offender in the community and "leveraging the family and community"
Hall	13	13	13	"I was much more flexible out of town; if you don't play ball, they'll shut down on you"; stressed the appropriateness of first and second chance for most offenders

Note: Incarceration and prison length ranks are in order of descending punitiveness (i.e., 1 = highest rate of incarceration and longest average length imposed). Number of offenders sentenced rank is in increasing order (i.e., 1 = fewest offenders sentenced).

for each punitiveness measure and were also the bottom three for fewest offenders sentenced.

Cross-Pollination and Sharing of Ideas

Rotation also facilitates the sharing of ideas, which pulls practices away from localizations and toward a more uniform, statewide legal culture. According to Judge Andrews, rotation prevented "disparity in customs and practices from county to county." He suggested that without rotation, "after 10 years the courthouse becomes the judge's fiefdom. The judge may or may not follow the rules of court, may or may not properly apply the rules of evidence, may or may not recognize hearsay objections; he or she may or may not suppress evidence when it's called for." By ensuring that attorneys see many judges, rotation provides a safety valve for the entrenched judge problem.

Judge Coleman explained that rotating into a large county where multiple judges sat during the same term allowed the judges to share ideas and philosophies. "When you go to [a particular large county], there'll be five judges from all different places. We have a chance to talk about sentencing policies. We might eat together, stay at the same motel, and really get to know each other. It's a bench that really gets to know each other." Judge Garland added: "You get to see how solicitors do things in different places and trade ideas. It's a good way to trade ideas." Similarly, Judge Hall suggested that "lawyers get a sense of variety with different judges—not for their entertainment or pleasure but to see new ideas, new people. It's refreshing and uplifting." If a new case-processing procedure or technology were to emerge and be effective, the traveling judges would transport the idea to other counties. Through this cross-pollination, new ideas spread across the state rather than remaining localized.

County Differences

While circuit rotation provides a gravitational force for sentencing culture norms, rotation does not extirpate all traces of unique county contributions to sentencing patterns. There are stark differences between some counties in terms of wealth, politics, culture, urbanization, and prosecutorial personalities. Since judges travel, they have a unique opportunity to observe contrasts between counties. When asked about divergent sentencing practices throughout the counties, judges revealed a variety of viewpoints, more so than on any other subject.

The general consensus was that while there were pronounced differences in social characteristics between counties across the state, they did not translate into divergences in sentencing offenders, thus confirming prior empirical findings (see the section "Judge and County Findings" in Chapter 3). Several judges noted that some procedural variations existed, particularly in how negotiations or recommendations were handled. In some jurisdictions, prosecutors might rely heavily on negotiated sentences or recommendations; in one jurisdiction, assistant solicitors have been instructed to make no recommendations. Judge Darnell gave the following example of differences in charge bargaining: "Some will have five charges and just sentence one or two, and others want to keep three or four of the five." But judges seemed to agree that these procedural variations make little difference in outcomes. As Judge Jenkins suggested, when they do threaten to create a discrepancy, "that's where you come in as the judge." In this judge's view, one of the roles of the traveling trial judge was to apply sentencing uniformly throughout the state and adjust for these procedural differences.

Procedural nuances aside, there were three exceptions where judges suggested that some meaningful variation existed: increased prosecutorial power in wealthier counties; cultural norms reflected in jury verdict patterns, which in turn affected pleas; and different priorities in drug cases. Several judges pointed out a different pattern in rural versus more populated counties, and all made the point that prosecutors in more urban areas sought more punitive sentences. The differences were driven by resources. According to Judge Lyndon, "More wealthy areas up the ante on time. Solicitors have to rely on county funding. In rural places, they just don't have the resources." Judge Iredell offered a similar assessment: "In the more populous and—I don't want to call them more sophisticated counties, but the ones with more money and more resources—the differences come out. The solicitor in [a large county] has many, many assistant solicitors, and so does the PD's [public defender's] office. Compared to [a rural county] where you might have one PD or a half a person hired part-time under contract.... In larger counties solicitors want more influence in helping you determine the sentence." Judge Hall concurred: "In [a larger county] they are stricter than in the smaller courts. Smaller counties tend to do a lot more [give up a lot more ground on sentences]." In the words of Judge Darnell, the clear theme was that prosecutors in rural counties with fewer resources "need to wholesale a lot of cases" and that therefore "different offers are made."

Judges also said pleas in some counties reflected the very different jury verdicts typically entered in those counties. According to Judge Andrews, "What might be a slam dunk conviction in one county might be a slam dunk not guilty verdict in another county. That has to affect plea negotiations." Judge Lyndon offered a similar observation: "In [one circuit], you might not have a single verdict of not guilty over the course of six months. Here [in the judge's home circuit], you might not get one conviction in six months. . . . It's about the background of your jury; the more wealthy, more educated juries [are more likely to convict]."

When judges were asked about variations in going rates across counties, most indicated that there were "not really" strong differences associated with county location and could not offer any examples. Two judges did provide concrete examples of substantive differences, both of which dealt with drug distribution. Judge Hall gave the following account:

> For example, in [County A] the sheriff took a hard stance on crack and cocaine, and the solicitor followed. So distribution of crack, first offense, might be 0–15 years, and there might be a small mandatory minimum with no suspended sentence allowed. In [County B] it'd be difficult to give two, three, four years on a distribution of crack first offense. (You know those cases are called distribution, but they aren't as bad as they sound. It's usually some crackh*** selling a rock to another crackh*** to get some for himself. It's not like major trafficking.) Well, anyway, in [County A] they are recommending 12 years, and the defense lawyers are begging the judge to take the 12.

Judge Lyndon gave a similar example: "In [County C, a specific rural county] if you're charged with distribution of crack cocaine, you may get a recommendation of 18 months to 3 years. You go to [County D, a specific large wealthy county] on the same offense, and the recommendation is 8 years."

Aside from these substantive patterns, there were several anecdotes about different regional sensibilities, but they seemed to be one-off stories with little generalizability to a jurisdiction or pattern as a whole. Judge Garland told the story of when he had been an assistant prosecutor and was presenting a judge with a recommendation for 20 years in prison for a murder.

> We were in chambers giving the judge the rundown, and the judge said, "Aw, hell, that ain't nothing but a hot supper killing." I didn't know exactly what he meant by "hot supper killing," but I gathered he didn't like our sentence and thought 20

years was too long. In fact, it was a Black on Black killing where the guys knew each other and things got heated, and the judge just didn't think it was worth 20 years; he thought it was worth more like 5 years. (Sometime later I ran into another judge from that area, and I asked him if he'd ever heard the phrase "hot supper killing,'" and he said, "oh yeah," he knew what that meant, so I guess that's something they said down there.)

Another judge gave an account (apocryphal, perhaps) that involved a rural community and what the judge called the "Hutchington Doctrine":

> Anything that has to do with intoxication, an altercation, or fornication, where both parties are from Hutchington, the crime is irrelevant. One Sunday afternoon, the people of that community were down by the river, having a fish fry, relaxing like they do on a Sunday afternoon. This one fellow gets to wondering where his wife wandered off to and goes out looking for her. Well, he sees some bushes moving over by the river bank, goes over and sees his best friend and his wife down in the bushes ... uh ... getting to know each other real well. So he gets a big stick and beats the guy with it. And he has to go down to the hospital, and this new deputy from the county who doesn't know about the Hutchington Doctrine charges the guy, and this young prosecutor who doesn't know about the Hutchington Doctrine comes and tries the case, and sure enough, it's an acquittal. The moral of the story is, if you know about the Hutchington Doctrine, don't waste your time.

More generally, drug sentencing seemed to be a particular area with less agreed-upon norms. Judge Coleman offered this explanation: "I came up on the bench when drugs became an issue. Nowadays, younger judges aren't as surprised by drugs. They grew up in an era where things were different [with respect to drug use]. Some of the older judges really had a different reaction to drugs because of the way things were socially when they were growing up. You're seeing that change now as the older judges retire and are replaced by younger judges." Judge Andrews, who described himself as "harsh" (and who was among the most punitive according to the data measures—see Table 4.1), proudly qualified that for drug offenses, he was actually quite lenient. He explained:

> On things like drug possession I am a light sentencer. I'll give you an example. The first time I ever went to [a particular county], my reputation preceded me. I got down there, and everyone was afraid to plead in front of me. But finally they got going a little bit, and we ended up holding court until 7:00 Friday night because all of these drug offenders wanted to plead in front of me. They got word that I was a lenient sentencer for these drug crimes. . . . These people get arrested in these poor, minority areas, not a pot to piss in, a ninth-grade education, and they get brought up on these distribution charges. The solicitor acts like they've got this big drug sting. Well, that drug sting is some poor person who gets arrested, and the police send them back to their neighborhood, and they convince all their friends to sell some drugs to them. So they're buying small amounts from their neighbors and what have you. Then here come the police on the news announcing a big bust of 30 or 40 "drug dealers." I mean, come on, everybody knows what's going on there. So for those cases a lot of times I'll just give credit for time served.

Yet Judge Andrews was quick to qualify that, "for true drug trafficking—where somebody is driving through on our interstates with a trunk full of drugs—now, I can't wait to sentence that person for as long as I can put them away for."

Discussion

This chapter turned to qualitative interviews with South Carolina trial judges to analyze the sentencing practices and legal culture of the state's court communities. The findings offer several contributions to the sentencing field: They advance the court communities literature by exploring system features that pull courts toward greater uniformity rather than diffusion, and they demonstrate the importance of a structural characteristic, judicial rotation, that has sentencing policy implications.

As a starting point, court literature establishes an expectation of large levels of variation in sentencing patterns among counties across a state. The courts as communities perspective offers a theoretical paradigm for these divergent practices, norms, going rates, and outcomes (Eisenstein et al., 1988). While sentencing guidelines could potentially affect these practices, even in guidelines jurisdictions, ground-level practitioners frequently find ways to circumvent new policy change to perpetuate the settled ways of doing things in that location. Where no guidelines are present to constrain, one would expect the inter-county differences to be even more drastic. However, South Carolina sentencing appears to exhibit notably less county variation in sentencing than has been observed in other jurisdictions.

The qualitative judge interview data used in this study explore a more statewide sentencing norm that pervades South Carolina. The results indicate that while some county-to-county differences certainly exist, the practice of judicial rotation exerts a normalizing force—a gravitational pull toward a more uniform state legal culture. The structural feature of rotation propagates this statewide culture through two distinct channels. First, rotation makes plea routing and judge shopping virtually inevitable. Second, rotation augments the interactions, networks, and what Eisenstein and colleagues call "grapevines"; judges have increased opportunities to interact with one another and with prosecutors and defense attorneys throughout the state, nurturing statewide legal culture.

As to the first mechanism, rotation creates options and opportunity for offenders. Scholars including Eisenstein and associates (1988) and Ulmer (1997) have previously highlighted the significance of judge shopping in the criminal court context. In other states, a local calendaring system might allow a savvy attorney to occasionally slip a case from one presiding judge to a more favorable one. In South Carolina, rotation invites defense counsel to judge shop in a monumental way by simply indicating a willingness to enter a plea at a strategic time (i.e., when a lenient judge is presiding) or using typical continuance and delay tactics to avoid a plea when a hanging judge is presiding. Judge shopping gives rise to the phenomenon of the plea judge, and plea judge norms influence the sentencing tendencies of some (though perhaps not all) of the other judges. Many judges become pragmatic sentencers; they are not predisposed to be lenient plea judges, but neither do they become entrenched hanging judges. Instead, the pragmatic judges exhibit a willingness to take recommendations or negotiations in accordance with the plea judge norms that offenders might otherwise hold out for. These typologies are illustrated by differences in willingness to accept recommended and negotiated pleas. For instance, attorneys apparently could trust that the plea judge, Judge Matthews, would impose an acceptable sentence; he indicated that he took straight pleas (i.e., pleas with no recommended sentence) at least 90 percent of the time. By stark contrast, Judge Darnell stated that straight pleas did not occur in front of him. He was "pragmatic," recognizing that "we need to move cases," and as a result accepted recommended or negotiated pleas in 80 percent to 90 percent of his cases.

As in all U.S. jurisdictions, cases in this state are predominantly disposed of through plea bargaining, though the small yet steady supply of trials takes up considerable court time. The rotation system allows prosecutors to maximize efficiency for everyone by assigning hanging judges to trial weeks and nonhanging judges to plea weeks. This tactic, which was frequently referred to in the interviews, fits in with the well-documented interdependent play among workgroup personnel (e.g., Eisenstein et al., 1988). Workgroup members are often said to engage in an informal sanctioning of a member who violates norms—for instance, "the defense attorney who violates routine cooperative norms may be punished by having to wait until the end of the day to argue his motion; he may be given less time than he wishes for a lunch break in the middle of a trial; he may be kept beyond usual court hours for bench conferences" (Eisenstein and Jacob, 1977, p. 27). In South Carolina, for the most entrenched hanging judges, the "sanctions" are either having defense counsel shut down on them or else having prosecutors assign the judges to trial weeks. All told, rotation, as an exaggerated example of a master calendaring system, leaves an indelible mark on sentencing practices.

In addition to the structural issues related to judge shopping, these findings reveal that rotation leads to norm spreading. As Judge Coleman noted, when several judges are holding court in one of the larger counties, they frequently spend time together socially and talk about the work of judging. In addition, judges experience interactions with a variety of attorneys from all parts of the state, which allows the judges and attorneys to see differences, "trade ideas," and "get a sense of variety." Nardulli, Eisenstein, and Flemming (1988) suggested that increased interactions might affect outcomes in dramatic ways; the South Carolina experience confirms their prediction (see also Eisenstein et al., 1988, pp. 50–51). Yet this gravitational pull toward homogenization is one of relative degree. South Carolina exhibits fewer intercounty variations than would be expected from a nonguidelines state, but some differences persist.

The judges identified a few county-specific characteristics that they believed constituted meaningful distinctions. These highlight the important point that rotation contributes to a more uniform, but not completely uniform, statewide culture. One example is the handling of drug cases and the pattern of prosecutorial influence toward more punitive sentences in the larger, more populous counties. While suggestive of county-level differences, these perceived variances from a few of the counties in their approach to specific drug issues are not so pronounced as to translate into wide variations when all of the county outcomes are pooled together. As noted from the prior multilevel findings, while outcomes are certainly not perfectly uniform across counties, the variation is relatively minimal.

The pattern of more punitive treatment in the larger counties is also interesting as it appears at odds with other court communities research that finds that courts in the largest jurisdictions actually impose more lenient sentences on offenders (see, e.g., Ulmer and Johnson's [2004] multilevel examination of court communities in Pennsylvania). One possible explanation for this discrepancy involves an intersection between the dominance of metropolitan centers and a critical mass of population in medium-sized jurisdictions. South Carolina's largest cities, Columbia and Charleston, are small compared to large urban centers like Philadelphia and Pittsburgh. Big-city mechanisms that influence leniency include things like desensitization to violent crime and high levels of bureaucratization in the face of exponentially larger case flows (e.g., Dixon, 1995). In contrast, South Carolina's most populous cities are big enough to create more powerful prosecutorial offices but not so substantial as to trigger the desensitization reactions of America's largest cities.

Given the significant differences that exist among judges, it is noteworthy that these judge-level differences failed to translate into larger levels of county-level variation. In part, this is explained by the strong influence of plea judge norms and the ability of prosecutors to route judges to plea courts or trials. Nevertheless, rotation is nonsystematic, and not every offender will be presented with the opportunity to defer a plea in front of a hanging judge one week for a plea judge the next. Yet even when judge-level differences manifest, rotation again plays the role of equalizer, distributing these judge-level differences across the counties as the judges travel.

Judge-level variation also raises the larger point that while increased interactions reportedly affected norms, it is not possible to determine the extent to which judge preferences were actually changed by interactions with other judges. There was some indication that judges did influence one another, as seen in Judge Coleman's comments that judges might discuss sentencing policies while interacting socially when on assignment in the same county. Certainly any influence toward a more uniform set of sentencing norms was not so extensive as to wash out all meaningful differences in the judges' approaches and sentencing philosophies. Eisenstein and colleagues (1988) theorized that such interactions would affect shared norms, and perhaps this is true in South Carolina. But substantial differences persist, giving rise to the plea judges and to the instrumental role of prosecutors and their decisions related to assigning judges to plea and trial sessions.

Increasingly, scholars have noted the importance of analyzing the role of prosecutors.[6] Prosecutors were reported to embrace the plea judge system for its ability to facilitate case-processing efficiency—one of the primary goals of all workgroup actors (Eisenstein and Jacob, 1977). The solicitors were also said to strategically use the rotation system to their advantage at times—for instance, by emphasizing to the defendant that a lenient judge was currently presiding but that a harsher judge might preside over a plea or trial at a later date. Further, prosecutors played an instrumental mediating role for the judge-shopping mechanism wherein the defense would shut down on harsh judges. Consistent with the idea that maintaining efficiency is a paramount concern, the data indicated that prosecutors used trial assignments to minimize shutdowns and to maximize the use of trial time resources.

However, the prosecutorial role was only indirectly examined through the judges' comments, and the data left many unanswered questions related to prosecutors in this jurisdiction. Interviews with the solicitors and their assistants would be better suited for discerning the degree to which these prosecutors were facilitating the plea routing or merely reacting to it and making the most of it given the reality of rotation. It was also unclear how other prosecutorial tools, such as mandatory minimum charging, affected the plea-bargaining dynamics here. It would be beneficial to examine how the system of rotation affected prosecutorial bargaining, dismissals, and other discretionary outcomes. Interviews with prosecutors are crucial for probing these significant questions, and research that pairs quantitative results with qualitative prosecutorial data would be a fruitful avenue for future research.

"Justice by geography" and the idea that location matters in sentencing have long raised fairness concerns among policymakers and scholars (see, e.g., Feld, 1991; Harries and Lura, 1974; Kramer and Ulmer, 2009). Indeed, the failure of like cases being treated alike across location was one of the several concerns used to justify the implementation of guidelines in many jurisdictions. There is mixed evidence on how successful guidelines have been in meeting their policy goals,[7] but one of the primary macrolevel theoretical contributions of the courts as communities theory is that the informal decisions of courtroom actors are just as important to shaping policy as are formal legal changes (such as the implementation of guidelines). This chapter has highlighted underdeveloped theoretical aspects of the communities perspective that show how structural changes can ultimately affect outcomes through indirect avenues of legal culture. While embracing the concept that informal legal culture affects sentencing, this chapter suggests that the informal culture may itself be shaped by policy decisions related to the structure of courts, mechanisms affecting the degree of interaction among judges and other courtroom actors, and perhaps even the judicial selection system.

The results presented in this chapter demonstrate some of the benefits of using qualitative data to enhance our understanding of sentencing processes. However, the study does have several limitations. Because South Carolina does not continually maintain statewide sentencing data, it is currently not possible to examine quantitatively how sentencing practices have changed over time. In addition, as mentioned, access to other members of the workgroup, particularly prosecutors but also defense counsel, would surely reveal enlightening accounts of sentencing practices and the nuances of court community norms.

What could other jurisdictions learn about sentencing and punishment reform from these findings? The results suggest that aside from sentencing guidelines, other mechanisms of structure and culture can achieve traditional sentencing reform goals like uniformity. While a full-blown statewide circuit rotation approach might not be a desirable reform for many states, narrower rotation programs or other calendaring strategies could expand the number of judges that preside in a given jurisdiction. In addition, policymakers in other jurisdictions could explore increasing the frequency and intensity of interactions and networking of workgroup actors, such as through more frequent judicial conferences and retreats. The results also suggest that new avenues of research might uncover other structures and mechanisms that lead to greater uniformity in legal culture and, consequently, in outcomes across a jurisdiction. These ideas and their implications are explored further in Chapters 6 and 7. In the next chapter, we turn to two additional key themes and potential lessons that emerged from the judge interviews—one relating to the role of prior record for purposes of current sentencing and the second exploring some of the reasons the sentencing guidelines movement seemed to fail in South Carolina despite the decades-long effort.

5

Judging Prior Record

This chapter continues with the exploration of the results of the judge interviews, focusing on perhaps the most immediately striking difference between the South Carolina quantitative findings and practices from sentencing guidelines jurisdictions: the use of defendant criminal history. Empirical sentencing research consistently cites prior record as one of the strongest predictors of punishment outcomes (though there are suggestions that the role of criminal history is more prominent in the United States than in some other Western jurisdictions; e.g., Lappi-Seppälä, 2011; Roberts and Sanchez, 2015). American scholars have considered criminal history an indispensable control in modeling sentencing decisions for half a century. Beginning in the late 1970s, sentencing guidelines systems formalized the role of prior record in punishment by making it one of the two determinants of the recommended sentence. As scholars have observed, "two legal variables—offense severity and prior record—are associated most strongly with sentencing outcomes" (Steffensmeier, Ulmer, and Kramer, 1998, p. 775), and "it is irrefutable that the primary determinants of sentencing decisions are the seriousness of the offense and the offender's prior criminal record" (Spohn, 2000, p. 481).

Yet, as discussed in Chapter 3, the empirical findings from South Carolina reveal that while criminal history was highly predictive of the decision to incarcerate, it was not a significant predictor of the sentence length determination (see also Hester and Hartman, 2017). Accordingly, the judge interviews also included some questions exploring the significance of prior record. Because these findings so poignantly contrast a potentially major difference in guidelines versus nonguidelines sentencing, this chapter also delves into a historical analysis of the guidelines formation literature to explain how and why guidelines came to feature the robust prior-record-based punishment premiums that are found in most structured sentencing systems (Frase et al., 2015).

The History of Criminal History

The first statewide sentencing guidelines were adopted in the early 1980s, with a sentencing grid as a defining feature. The grids harnessed two dimensions—offense severity and prior record—to structure punishment ranges. These early statewide systems often gathered data on past sentencing practices but formulated their own punishment recommendations in a prescriptive fashion (Knapp, 1982; Kramer and Ulmer, 2009). Yet they adopted the two-dimensional grid approach seemingly as part and parcel of the decision to develop guidelines. How the two-dimensional grid came to be has largely been forgotten in the story of structured sentencing reform and potentially has important substantive implications for the prominent role that prior record has come to play in modern sentencing.

Exploring these issues of the origins of guidelines and the practices of nonguidelines judges answers the call for more research in nonguidelines jurisdictions (e.g., Engen, 2009). Guidelines research has dominated the sentencing field for the past several decades (Ulmer, 2012). Prior record is indisputably a highly predictive factor in states where the guidelines have prescribed its role as a determinative factor. (In fact, prior record effects are often found in guidelines research even when controlling for the presumptive or recommended sentence.) But two-thirds of U.S. states continue to operate without guidelines (Frase, 2019), creating a "dark area" in our understanding of how sentencing operates in most of the United States.

Further, although criminal history is often regarded as a legitimate "legal" characteristic, in recent years, scholars have raised concerns about its mediating effect on racial disparities (Frase, 2009; Tonry, 1993; Ulmer, Painter-Davis, and Tinik, 2016) as well as other consequences that flow from criminal history enhancements. Under most sentencing guidelines, an offender's past criminal record can count more toward the prison sentence than the crime for which they are being sentenced, not just for felonies but also for misdemeanors, juvenile offenses, and custody status violations. In some states, an offender's record alone can increase the recommended sentence by 1,000 percent or more (Hester, Frase, Roberts, and Mitchell, 2018).

The Significance of Prior Record at Sentencing

During the 1970s and 1980s, many states began adopting structured sentencing reforms that would dramatically affect sentencing scholarship, creating a "new wave" of research based on administrative sentencing data collected by commissions using new computer-based case management systems (Zatz, 1987). Subsequently, prior record was taken for granted as a legitimate legal characteristic that should rightly affect punishment. It was operationalized into one of the two structural dimensions of sentencing guidelines in the earliest guidelines states (e.g., Minnesota, Pennsylvania, Maryland, Washington), and many subsequent commissions followed suit. Under these new guidelines, dispositions for incarceration time were determined by the severity of the offense and prior record. The duration of the sentence was likewise determined by severity and prior record, with punishments for a given severity level increasing in a linear fashion with each increase in prior record score. Criminal history's role in sentencing was also largely taken for granted by scholars who considered it a legal characteristic and a necessary control variable (e.g., Steffensmeier, Ulmer, and Kramer, 1998, p. 775). It became "irrefutable that the primary determinants of sentencing decisions are the seriousness of the offense and the offender's prior criminal record" (Spohn, 2000, p. 481).

The prior record's preeminent role in guidelines jurisdictions does appear irrefutable, and as scholars have repeatedly noted, most contemporary sentencing research derives from sentencing guidelines jurisdictions (Engen, 2009). However, more than half of the states continue to operate without guidelines. As explored in Chapter 3, the empirical results from South Carolina indicate that while criminal history was one of the strongest predictors of whether an offender received probation or prison, it was marginal or not statistically significant for the determination of sentence length, depending on modeling decisions. The minimal significance of prior record to sentence length offered a stark contrast to the substantial premiums built into sentencing guidelines. On first pass, these findings seem like aberrations. If prior record is universally one of the most salient predictors of sentence severity, why would it not be so in nonguidelines jurisdiction? However, it is also possible that those results were consistent with preguidelines practices and only seem aberrant because the guidelines imposed sentence increases to an extent that did not always reflect preguidelines sentencing.

There are additional indications from the literature that, in the absence of guidelines, prior record does not have the same import for the length decision as it does for the in/out decision. Studies using the State Court Processing Statistics (SCPS) provide mixed results. Anne Piehl and Shawn Bushway (2007) compared sentencing in Maryland and Washington and found that prior felonies were a statistically significant predictor in both states; serving a prior jail term was not significant in either state; and serving a prior prison term was significant under the presumptive Washington guidelines but not the advisory Maryland guidelines. Xia Wang and colleagues (2013) also found mixed prior record results when disaggregating the SCPS data by jurisdiction sentencing structure type (presumptive guidelines, voluntary guidelines, or no guidelines). For the incarceration disposition model, the criminal record variable was not statistically significant for jail (relative to probation) in nonguidelines or voluntary guidelines states but was in presumptive guidelines jurisdictions; it was statistically significant for prison (relative to probation) in all three jurisdiction types. For the length model, the criminal record was not significant for prison length in any of the three jurisdiction types, consistent with the Hester and Hartman (2017) findings. Other SCPS studies, however, have found significant prior record effects for both in/out and length decisions. Stephen Demuth and Steffensmeier (2004) and Wang and Daniel Mears (2015) combined prior arrests, prior convictions, prior jail incarcerations, and prior prison incarcerations into a single measure. Though most guidelines account for several dimensions of prior record, most do not incorporate arrests or prior incarcerations (Frase et al., 2015). In addition, differences between guidelines and nonguidelines jurisdictions were not a focus for either study; thus it is possible that strong prior record effects in guidelines jurisdictions drove the pooled effects.

Other research suggests that the importance of prior record may be conditional on the location and question of interest and therefore not irrefutably a determinative characteristic of all punishment outcomes. In Martin Levin's (1972, p. 102) classic (preguidelines) study on urban politics, he noted that "in Minneapolis defendants with a prior record receive much more severe sentences than those without one. This pattern does not occur in Pittsburgh sentencing." Susan Welch and Cassia Spohn's (1986) study of sentencing in seven cities from 1968 to 1979 examined a number of different prior record measures, which included things like binary indicators and counts of misdemeanor convictions, felony arrests, felony convictions, and incarceration sentences. They found that the various measures of prior record did not always correlate with one another to a strong degree and that for the in/out decision, some prior record measures were reasonably good predictors. They concluded: "On the whole, none of our prior record measures did particularly well in predicting sentence severity, except for measures of incarceration, which we had from only one city" (Welch and Spohn, 1986, p. 398).

In summary, prior record is undoubtedly one of the key factors for some aspects of sentencing, even absent guidelines. However, there is evidence that trial judges—at least some judges in some places—historically used information related to prior record differently for the decisions of whether to incarcerate and how long to incarcerate. These nuances have been lost in the emphatic generalizations that prior record is one of the strongest predictors of punishment. It is possibly more accurate that prior record was almost always one of the strongest predictors of the in/out decision and was sometimes, but not always, a strong predictor of the length decision. Of course, the generalization of the role of prior record in less structured sentencing systems became a moot point for research under sentencing guidelines once it was formally given a determinative impact on both of the two traditional sentencing outcomes, which invites the question of how the guidelines came to be.

Content Analysis: Guidelines Formation Reports

Consistent with Mona Lynch and Alyse Bertenthal's (2016) historical analysis of the federal guidelines' criminal history score, the first stage of analysis for the current project involves an examination of the earliest guidelines formation materials. This section documents (1) how and why sentencing guidelines took on a grid matrix form in the first place and (2) how and why prior record came to occupy one of the two determinative elements of the grid. While Lynch and Bertenthal (2016) recount how the federal criminal history score came to be, they leave unaddressed the integration of criminal history into guidelines before the federal system was installed. By the time the federal guidelines took effect in 1987, several jurisdictions (Minnesota, Pennsylvania, Washington, Maryland) had already been using a statewide grid-based guidelines system for more than half a decade (Frase, 2019). The grid structure and criminal history operationalizations ultimately adopted by the U.S. Commission were derivative of the similar grids and scores from other jurisdictions that had been in place for years.

For this analysis, I identified a series of early guidelines formation reports and evaluations,[1] mostly associated with a federally funded project spearheaded by Don M. Gottfredson, Leslie T. Wilkins, Peter Hoffman, Jack Kress, and colleagues. Those documents provide an account of how a movement toward more structured decision-making led to a parole release matrix that provided a blueprint for sentence decision-making.

From Back-End Parole Decisions to Front-End Sentencing Decisions

During the 1960s, a team of researchers were at work on actuarial instruments that could predict recidivism and inform the parole decision-making process (see, e.g., Gottfredson and Ballard, 1965; Gottfredson and Beverly, 1962). This eventually culminated in the Federal Parole Board's adoption of the Salient Factor Score in the early 1970s (e.g., Calpin et al., 1982; Hoffman and Beck, 1974). Although the same federal Sentencing Reform Act of 1984 that would give birth to the U.S. Sentencing Commission would also end parole in the federal system, in the meantime the concept of parole release guidelines took hold in federal practice and spread to a number of other jurisdictions. By the early 1970s, these efforts at structuring parole decisions were seen as a success, and the same team set its sights on the front-end sentencing process.[2] As Carrow and colleagues (1985, p. 29) indicated, "'The concept of guidelines for sentencing seemed a natural extension of the idea as applied in the parole timesetting decisions,' according to Wilkins."

The new guidelines project began with a 1974 feasibility study funded by the National Institute of Law Enforcement and Criminal Justice, followed by a second phase in 1976 for development and implementation in four pilot sites (Calpin et al., 1982, p. iii). Along with Gottfredson, who was then dean of the School of Criminal Justice at Rutgers, Albany University professors Wilkins and Kress were codirectors of various aspect of the project. The feasibility research produced a methodology of developing guidelines descriptively on past practices, which became known as the "Albany method" (see Knapp, 1982) because their research operations were based at the Albany Criminal Justice Research Center (Carrow et al., 1985).

From its inception, the guidelines team seemed inexorably drawn to the grid approach those same researchers previously had relied on in the parole guidelines development. As is clear from the first pages of one of the feasibility study reports, the researchers were propelled by the assumption that a decision matrix would be central to sentencing guidelines. They explored several preliminary models, but "each . . . employed some form of a two dimensional decision-making grid or matrix" (Wilkins et al., 1978, p. 15).

These early architects recognized that sentencing guidelines would differ from parole guidelines because sentencing involved the two distinct decisions of whether to imprison and, if so, for how long (Calpin et al., 1982). Parole decision-making, by contrast, only involved the question of when to release (Wilkins et al., 1978). Given the complexities of balancing accuracy and parsimony, along with the political feasibility of implementing guidelines that were seen as encroachments on judicial discretion, the researchers sought to develop a single instrument that would accommodate both decisions. However, the pilot guideline development documents suggest that a single instrument did not always neatly accommodate both decisions. The Albany approach involved an empirical process of relating potential sentencing factors to the sentencing outcomes on the basis of the recent past practices in a given jurisdiction. The researchers would then trim away the most extreme sentences so that recommended ranges reflected the central 80 percent or so of sentences as a way to increase uniformity and consistency in sentencing. Between the two outcomes of disposition and duration, the architects viewed the in/out decision as primary because it determined whether there would be a loss of liberty (Wilkins et al., 1978). Since the decision was made to use a single grid, and since in/out was the predominant decision, grids were first constructed on the basis of past in/out practices. Average sentence lengths would then be overlaid for each cell. Problematically, in several jurisdictions, relying on past sentence length averages to populate recommended prison ranges did not create a cohesive, linear system. In Cook County, analysis revealed that "individual cells which did not conform to the overall pattern, that is, increasing offense and offenders scores are paralleled by increasing sentence severity" (Calpin et al., 1982, p. 76). As a result, "mapping the length of sentences was not predictive in the statistical sense. Thus, the guideline model became an 'experience' table" (p. 76). As another example, Calpin and colleagues (1982) report correlation coefficients among 21 prospective criminal history variables and the outcomes (in/out and length) for Maricopa County. Of these, all but two held a statistically significant relationship with the in/out decision (and even these two were marginally significant at .057 and .093). But only four of the 21 variables were related to the minimum and maximum length outcomes at statistically significant levels. The final model for Maricopa included four criminal history measures: two that were related to all outcomes and two that were only statistically significant for disposition.

A 1978 external evaluation by the National Center for State Courts (NCSC) criticized the efforts for not creating two grids based on two sets of factors to separately accommodate the in/out and length decisions (Carrow et al., 1985, p. 34). According to Carrow and colleagues (1985, p. 42n39), "The NCSC evaluators contended that sentences cannot be captured accurately by one matrix using the same variables and weights and predicting both decisions. Indeed, the evaluators found that the determinates of the decision to incarcerate differed from the determinants of length of incarceration." Criminal history was listed as one of the best predictors of the in/out decisions but not as one of the best predictors of the sentence length decision (those were instead offense severity, injury to the victim, presence of charge reductions, mode of conviction, and number of counts). By the time of these observations, the grid movement was well under way, and the two-dimensional matrix was already a staple of structured sentencing reform.

Descriptive Guidelines and Prescriptive Guidelines

At a minimum, these examples suggest that the preguidelines relationship between prior record and sentence length was not universally the uniform, linear relationship that was ultimately encoded into guidelines grids. Instead, in at least some instances, linear increases were overlaid to present a single matrix that made sense for both disposition and duration. Elsewhere, other nascent guidelines efforts were formulating linear prior record enhancements for different reasons. In the last years of the 1970s, as the descriptive Albany-method project was cementing the grid approach, state commissions began work on statewide guidelines. Several of the earliest and most enduring guidelines systems, Minnesota, Pennsylvania, and Washington, departed from the descriptive approach in favor of a prescriptive approach in which the commission prescribed policy apart from whatever past practices had been. Both Washington and Minnesota, for example, were influenced by the reemerging emphasis on retribution spearheaded by von Hirsch (1976) and the associated view that punishment should be increased as criminal history increased on grounds of retribution (see Boerner, 1985; Parent, 1988). Although von Hirsch later augmented his views on how prior record affects desert (von Hirsch 2010), the monotonic criminal history premiums that his early views inspired became ossified. And while some of the early commissions engaged in prescriptive policymaking that may have wittingly inflated prior record premiums over past practices, it is possible that even these approaches were influenced by the suggestiveness of the grid approach introduced in the body of work by Gottfredson and colleagues.

Qualitative Interview Study

Since the findings from South Carolina are so divergent on the role of prior record as compared to that feature's usage in guidelines jurisdictions, the judge interviews (introduced in Chapter 4) included questions probing the role of prior record. The interviews began with an open-ended question on the judges' approaches to sentencing. To provide the appropriate context for the prior record findings, the results begin with the presentation of answers related to the broader approach to sentencing before moving to the role of criminal history.

The Judges' Sentencing Philosophies

The judges were initially asked to describe their approaches to sentencing and to identify the factors or case attributes they found most important for determining an appropriate sanction. The gravity and difficulty of the task of identifying an appropriate sentence emerged as a common theme. Judges noted that there frequently was no clear answer for how to sentence, especially for the length of prison term to impose. "Often there is no right answer," Judge Case explained. "Like six months versus eight months—what's the value of an extra two months? It's not always clear what's right. It's not a science. It's very, very difficult." Judge Edwards raised similar issues: "Why do you pick a number of years?" he reflected. "Why four versus five? Why do you do what you do?" Many of the judges noted that sentencing could be "very subjective" and stressed the "intangible" aspect that required the judge to "go with your gut." Judge Florence summarized: "In all of these years I've never become completely comfortable with it [sentencing], and I hope I never do, hope I never become uncaring or calloused about it."

The judges shared many aspects of sentencing philosophy in common. All of the judges discussed the severity or nature of the offense as being paramount, and almost all mentioned the defendant's prior record. While these common denominators emerged, there were differences in whether the judges thought certain extralegal characteristics were pertinent to the sentencing decision. Seven of the judges specifically mentioned the importance of factors like the age of the offender, social and economic situations, work history, dependent children, family, and support structure. In most cases, these emerged as mitigating factors, characteristics that might lead a judge to give a community sentence rather than prison. But this was not always the case. For example, Judge Keys's account of some social factors did not reflect mitigation: "Some things I don't pay much attention to. Like family and children. I don't really consider that as mitigating. If anything, it's almost aggravating for me. If you had those things in your life, you should have been that much more careful not to have committed this crime." Judge Florence also gave an example of the negative influence that lack of family support could have:

> You look at the individual, their age, education, vocation, community support. One of the more important things for me is family and community support. It really troubles me when you have a young, 20-year-old man, often African American, come before you on a burglary charge where they could get 10 years and no one shows up with them but the PD [public defender].
> [The judge asks:] "Where's mama?"
> [The defendant answers:] "At work."
> [The judge asks:] "Where's daddy?"
> [The defendant answers:] "I don't know my daddy."
> That really bothers me.

While just over half of the judges discussed extralegal characteristics, almost as many did not volunteer them as being important.

One lenient judge stressed the importance of community; he would frequently give offenders prison sentences suspended on 90 days to be served on the weekends. (In this jurisdiction, any active sentence over 90 days is served under custody of the state corrections system, while any sentence 90 days or less is served in a local jail.) "So my general philosophy," Judge Maurus explained, "is keep them in the community. You do 90 days, 2 days at a time on the weekend for 45 weeks—that'll really cut into somebody's drug habit, you know?" The 90-day split-time sentence would allow the offender to remain in the community, keep his or her job, and maintain family and other community ties.

Several judges made a point of the benefits of maintaining community support where practicable, but as Judge Keys and several others observed, receiving a "lenient" suspended sentence could be deceptive. Judge Maurus regularly warned defendants:

> I always tell them, if you are getting an eight-year prison sentence suspended on five years' probation, you are really getting a thirteen-year sentence. And you are getting the most due process you are ever going to get. You can go and live out all but one day of those five years' probation, but if you mess up on that last day, you'll go away and serve that eight-year sentence. And there won't be a trial or a bunch of due process or this long recitation of your rights—next time you'll just get sent away.

Many of the judges interviewed specifically gave the same example of Judge Jones, who famously gave defendants the maximum sentence permitted suspended on five years' probation (the maximum term of probation generally allowed in the state). While this practice had a dimension of leniency since offenders initially avoided prison, one respondent claimed that Judge Jones had more prisoners serving active sentences than any other judge in the state because so many would inevitably violate their probation, and when they did, they went to prison for the statutory maximum term, which was much longer than what other judges would have sentenced them to in the first place. And although Judge Jones's exceptional practice was not emulated by others on the same scale, the point remained: a "lenient" probation sentence that, if violated, could trigger a long prison term with few if any intervening due process opportunities is not always as lenient as it first appears.

The Relevance of Prior Record

Most of the judges raised some aspect of prior record while answering the open-ended question about their general approach to sentencing. When they did, additional questions were asked to delve deeper into when and why an individual's prior record mattered. In the few instances that judges did not initially volunteer anything about criminal history, a follow-up question about prior record was asked. The interviews converged around three themes related to prior record. First, many of the judges expressed a strong preference for treating first-time offenders differently. Second, most judges were careful to point out that their assessment of prior record was not mechanical but more general and holistic. They were interested in patterns of offending, gaps between offenses, and so forth. Third, several discussed custody status (i.e., being on probation or parole when the current offense was committed), but not always in the typical way guidelines handle it. These judges emphasized the positive signals of successful completion of probation and parole, not just the negative signals of failure.

Second Chances

Most judges thought that first- and second-time offenders should not be sent to prison unless the offense was violent or very serious but that at some point, a custodial sentence became justified. Although the judges did not typically speak in overtly philosophical terms, the preference for second and third chances for nonviolent offenders seemed to be tied to a utilitarian approach. In the words of Judge Hill:

> Except for violent cases—murder, robbery, etc., I always feel like the defendant should be given a first chance every time—that's for things like shoplifting, drugs, burglary. It's good to give probation and give them a second chance. Plus, it's just impossible to lock everybody up; we just can't do it. And maybe probation a second time, plus maybe 10 or 20 days in jail just to give them a taste. But by the third time, you're about ready to stop messing around with this and let them spend some time in jail.

Judge Jennings shared a similar perspective: "If it's shoplifting, and if they've had five shoplifting convictions in the past, then whatever we've done in the past is not working." Even the most lenient judges, like Judge Keys, noted that a persistent string of offending signaled that "we haven't gotten this person's attention yet; they need some kind of confinement or loss of liberty." Judge Armstrong specifically tied second chances to rehabilitation. "We work hard at rehabilitation," he said. "So most first and second offenders get probation. But if it's the fourth or fifth time for this person, I don't see a chance of rehabilitation anymore."

Not Just the Number of Checks against Them

A related finding was that the type and timing of the priors were key indicators of the significance of the record. Stale offenses carried less weight, while fresh offenses were more salient. In addition, judges noted that prior record was more important for the in/out decision than the length decision. Judge Maurus couched this observation in the language of deterrence: "Prior record goes not as much to the severity as the certainty. . . . You know a lot of times there's not a lot of difference between 15 and 20 years."

Once a person crossed a judge's threshold, some custody time became appropriate, but the judges were careful to point out that the manner in which they considered prior offenses was selective. For Judge Taylor, the offender's criminal history was "not important for all crime." Instead, the judge said, "When I'm talking about priors, I'm looking for a pattern, not just any type of prior." In particular, a minor and unrelated offense, a big gap between the last offense and the current one, or an offense committed by a juvenile would not necessarily be considered. Judge McGill made the similar point that a person's prior offenses were not mechanically counted: "It's not just the number of checks against them. It goes more deeply. Were they on probation? Did they live probation? How long has it been? Have you gone 10 years without getting into trouble? Do they have any crimes of violence? If it's a drug case, what are the amounts, etc." Judge Williams also stressed that while prior record could be "very important," the circumstances mattered. For him, it depended on "the nature and frequency and recency." He was also interested in how long they had "survived" after a prior parole or prison release. "Did they survive just a week, or did they make it five years?" Judge Chapman too brought up the gap between offenses: "And I look at the time between offenses. If it's 2015 and they haven't had an offense since 2000—it says something not to fall off for 15 years."

Living One

Whether a person had previously been a success or failure with probation was highly relevant to many of the judges. Judge Shires explained, "I always want to know what it [the prior offense] was and the disposition—did they get an active sentence or probation, which would tell me if they could live one." "Living one," referred to "living out a probation sentence," or successfully completing the probation terms without violating them. For Judge Shires and several others, "if they couldn't live one before, they probably can't now," but if they were successful on probation before, perhaps they could be again. Judge Florence stated that if an offender had successfully completed probation before, that was a good indicator that another probationary sentence might be appropriate, even if the offender had been on probation several times. "If they've been on probation in the past, I'm always interested in how they did. If they flunked and got revoked, it's unlikely I'll try again. But if they were on their third time on probation and did OK, I might give it again." The issue was not whether an offender failed to learn long-term lessons but whether, at least for the duration of probation, the offender knew how to conform to the rules of law when supervised and was thus considered amenable to probation.

Policy Implications

The accounts of these judges offer several insights. First, the results shed some light on how prior records affected the two sentencing outcomes differently for these judges. Second, they offer some additional support for revisiting the supposed truism that prior record is always one of the two primary determinants of sentencing decisions. Beginning with the narrower issue of explaining the prior quantitative results from this state, these qualitative findings are consistent with previous observations that sentencing involves two distinct decisions: whether to incarcerate and, if so, for how long. These judges had much to say about how prior record might affect the in/out decision. Judges were in favor of giving all but the most serious offender a second or even third chance before resorting to incarceration. This preference helps to explain why criminal history was such a strong predictor of the decision to incarcerate in the previous research. The interviews did not reveal a well-formulated connection between sentencing purposes and outcomes or indicate how differences in perceptions of blameworthiness or public safety risk might play out differently for one sentencing decision but not the other. One of the more commonly held perspectives was for first- (maybe even second- and third-) offender mitigation: absent an egregious crime, most judges preferred to avoid a loss of liberty for the novice. Eventually, persistence in even low-level offending would signal to most judges that some loss of liberty was appropriate. These findings are consistent with a strong relationship between prior record and the incarceration decision. In contrast, the judges offered little to suggest that they viewed a count of prior offenses as linearly related to the length of the prison term for those incarcerated. To the contrary, many of the judges stressed that the role of prior record was not mechanical, that it was not "just the number of checks" against a person. Instead, judges considered a variety of information related to offending and reoffending patterns, including the nature of the priors, the length of time since the last offense, the offender's age at the time of the priors, and the offender's demonstration of the ability to successfully "live" a probation or parole sentence.

Apart from the nonmechanical use of prior record, several of these judges indicated that sentence length determinations were somewhat arbitrary. Some judges reflectively asked what the differences were in eight months versus six months or five years versus four. These comments are particularly interesting in light of the growing body of literature suggesting that increasing the length of prison terms provides little or no additional specific deterrent effects and may even have criminogenic effects (Mitchell et al., 2017).

Criminal history has repeatedly been identified as one of the most important predictors of sentencing. But a second look at some of the nonguidelines sentencing studies, including some of the accounts of the formation of the earliest guidelines, indicates that prior record's relevance—for sentence length determinations—may have been conditional all along. There are several pieces of empirical and historical work that support this more nuanced account. These include some of the early guidelines formation documents (e.g., Calpin et al., 1982; Wilkins et al., 1978; see also Minnesota Sentencing Guidelines Commission, 1980, p. 5), as well as work by scholars including Welch and Spohn (1986) and mixed findings from studies using SCPS data.

It could be that the earliest guidelines efforts inadvertently set the stage for an approach to criminal history that resulted in increased prison terms with insufficient justification. At least some of the earliest guidelines were presented as descriptive and billed as having been constructed through the Albany approach—a system that created guidelines based on the central tendencies of the past practices of judges. By creating recommendations that tightened the ranges of recommended sentences around past averages, the guidelines would rein in some judicial excesses and create a more uniform system of sentencing, one of the primary selling points of guidelines. Yet, as the guideline formation documents show, some of these purportedly descriptive efforts departed from past practices on the length recommendations to advance a simpler, parsimonious sentencing paradigm. To be sure, some early commissions made the decision to go beyond the descriptive approach and engage in a prescriptive policymaking under which prior record premiums were inspired by the resurgence of retributive theory and the position at that time of von Hirsch (Boerner, 1985; Parent, 1988). But already by this time the springboard for prescriptive grids was the descriptive grid approach. We cannot know how history might have turned out differently if the earliest guidelines had used multiple grids for the multiple decisions or used a non-grid guideline system such as those adopted in other nations (see Roberts, 2019).

During much of past few decades of guidelines-dominated research, prior record has been taken for granted as one of the two irrefutable determinates of sentencing. In more recent years, however, scholars have raised issues about the deleterious effects of prior record punishment premiums. Prior record enhancement policies have a disproportionate effect on African American offenders, who, on average, have more extensive prior records than white offenders (Ulmer, Painter-Davis, and Tinik, 2016). Frase and Hester (2019), extending Frase's (2009) prior work, found that prior record enhancements accounted for a substantial portion—sometimes the largest portion—of racial disparity introduced at the sentencing phase in guidelines jurisdictions. It is possible that guidelines actually build in a racial disadvantage through prior record premium policies for sentence length—the very opposite outcome commissions were aiming for in promulgating guidelines. Ryan King (2019) ties a substantial portion of the prison boom to rising criminal history scores, and Frase and colleagues have outlined other problematic aspects of prior record policies related to proportionality, the size and expense of prison populations, and the confounding results of such policies imposing the most punishment on offenders who may be nearing the end of their criminal careers (Hester, Frase, et al., 2018). The "Type B" discretionary decisions policymakers have made regarding prior record (in contrast to "Type A" discretion exercised by individual system actors) are being seen in a new light (see Bushway and Forst, 2013).

The connections between prior record, guidelines, and actuarial risk assessment are also worth contemplating. Although risk assessment at sentencing is controversial, the Model Penal Code on Sentencing recommends that commissions incorporate risk tools into the sentencing process (Reitz and Klingele, 2019). Information from risk assessments is incorporated into presentence investigation reports in a number of jurisdictions, and in a few states, including Virginia and Pennsylvania, an actuarial risk assessment is formally a part of the guidelines (see Hester, 2019b, 2020; Hyatt et al., 2011). For example, the Pennsylvania Commission on Sentencing received a legislative mandate in 2010 to develop a risk tool for use at sentencing. The commission endeavored for the better part of a decade and in 2019 adopted a risk instrument it had developed itself. The commission's instrument includes as predictors age, gender, current offense type, multiple current convictions, and three prior record measures: number of prior convictions, prior conviction type, and adjudication as a juvenile (205 Pa. Code Ch. 305 [2019]). A risk score will be calculated for every offender sentenced under the guidelines. Offenders scored low risk or high risk by the tool will be flagged for "Additional Information Recommended," with the guidelines recommending that the court consider additional information, including a more advanced risk and needs assessment, prior to sentencing (see 205 Pa. Code Ch. 305 [2019]).

Prior record is a primary factor in the Pennsylvania tool, as in most risk instruments, raising questions about the interplay among criminal history, risk, and guidelines. Some commentators have noted that the guidelines prior record score (PRS) effectively functions as a crude risk proxy (Hester, Frase, Laskorunsky, and Mitchell, 2019), yet it may do so imprecisely. Hester (2019a) conducted survival analysis on a cohort of over 130,000 Pennsylvania offenders and found that the guidelines PRS did not fully reflect differences in the likelihood of recidivism. There were clear differences in recidivism likelihood among first offenders and all others, but the differences in recidivism among other PRS categories were modest, and in one case there was no difference in recidivism rates between PRS categories. Using receiver operatorship characteristic analysis, Hester found that PRS was a poor recidivism predictor at .59 (meaning that between a randomly drawn nonrecidivist and a randomly drawn recidivist, the recidivist would have a higher PRS 59 percent of the time—a low level of discrimination considering that a coin toss would be correct 50 percent of the time). Further, if instead of the eight-category PRS the guidelines adopted a binary indicator that only distinguished between first offenders and those with any record, the AUC statistic would drop by just 1 percent, from .59 to .58. If the guidelines PRS is being utilized mostly as a risk proxy, redeveloping the score as an actuarial risk predictor would almost certainly result in more accurate identification of recidivists, a prospect that may be particularly interesting for jurisdictions contemplating ways to incorporate risk information in the sentencing process. However, there are at the same time numerous concerns about the appropriateness of risk predictions at the punishment stage, as well as concerns about the overuse of criminal history in sentencing outcomes (Frase and Roberts, 2019), so the desired role of both risk and prior record in punishment merits continued research and debate.

Whatever one's position on actuarial risk assessment, both the quantitative data (Chapter 3) and qualitative data (this chapter) from South Carolina suggest that judges, in the absence of guidelines, view the role of prior record quite differently from the role criminal history is prescribed by sentencing commissions. Prior record does seem to play a strong part in judicial in/out incarceration decisions, but the mechanical and linear punishment increases in sentence length dictated by guidelines are not reflective of the way these judges considered criminal history. Given the considerable negative unintended consequences that flow from guidelines' prior record policies, these results may provide commissions with safe harbor evidence to support dialing back their prior record enhancements.

6

The Conundrum of Punishment Reform

Tension between Uniformity and Discretion

In 1973 Judge Marvin Frankel called the sentencing power given to judges "terrifying and intolerable for a society that professes devotion to the rule of law" and ultimately denounced indeterminacy as law without order (p. 5). After almost half a century of sentencing reform, Tonry (2016) pronounced that "American sentencing is a disaster—unjust, unprincipled, arbitrary, overly severe, and absurdly expensive" (p. 1). Andrew Ashworth (1995) has likened sentencing to a cafeteria system where judges are allowed to pick and choose which justifications or rationales will apply at the moment (see also Bagaric, 2000). Sentencing may still say as much about the judge as the defendant. The high potential for a lack of uniformity is concern enough, but if there is little confidence in uniformity, then concerns over systematic racial bias in outcomes are even more salient. Our grappling with the Aristotelian command to treat like cases alike and different cases differently persists.

The previous chapters establish that South Carolina was able to achieve a surprising level of uniformity, compared even to sentencing guidelines jurisdictions. What is more, by not adopting guidelines, the state avoided problematic policy consequences that flow from the overreliance on prior record in sentencing that has been uncovered in guidelines jurisdictions (Frase et al., 2015). This chapter considers how other jurisdictions, including sentencing guidelines jurisdictions, could integrate lessons from South Carolina to realize progress toward justice in sentencing. The second part of the chapter draws on neoinstitutional theory to offer exportable ideas that stem from the South Carolina case study. Before delving into those recommendations, however, the first half of the chapter spotlights the need, even in guidelines jurisdictions, to continue striving toward sentencing uniformity and legitimacy.

Sentencing Guidelines Uniformity and Departure Discretion

There are indications that racial disparities have declined since the onset of the sentencing reform movement (R. King and Light, 2019) and that guidelines appear to increase uniformity and allow prison population control without sacrificing public safety (Frase, 2013; Ostrom et al., 2008; Reitz, 2005; Stemen et al., 2005). However, successful guidelines must also navigate the second half of the Aristotelian maxim: They must ensure some sufficient level of discretion to allow judges to treat different cases differently. The federal guidelines were derided for their complexity and rigidity (e.g., Frase and Mitchell, 2019; Stith and Cabranes, 1998; Tonry, 2016), including what commentators have generally regarded as overly restrictive departure standards. In almost all of the successful state systems, departures from the guidelines serve as a key mechanism for balancing discretion and uniformity. As Frase has observed, even in the guidelines systems with the largest bodies of appellate law reviewing departures, like Kansas, Minnesota, Oregon, and Washington, "trial courts retain considerable discretion as to both the type and the severity of sanctions.... Appellate review does not appear to have unduly limited trial court discretion" (Frase, 2019, p. 99). Elsewhere, Frase (1994, p. 175) elaborates:

> Even within the group of states with presumptively binding guidelines, standards for departure and appellate review vary widely. In Pennsylvania, for example, departures are rarely reversed except on procedural grounds (failure to state reasons),

whereas reversal on substantive grounds (improper sentence) often occurs in Alaska, Washington, and Minnesota, each of which has a large body of substantive appellate caselaw. Nevertheless, trial courts in these states still retain substantial areas of discretion regarding both the type and severity of sanctions. In this respect, the federal guidelines appear to be uniquely and unnecessarily rigid.

Indeed, rather than imparting too much rigidity, it is possible that guidelines deliver too little uniformity because of departure policies, though this is an issue that, until now, has not been adequately examined.

The next section investigates an unexplored yet crucial aspect of evaluating sentencing guidelines for their ability to impart uniformity and sentencing and also underscores the need for guidelines jurisdictions to continue their efforts in striving for uniformity in sentencing. We begin with an examination of uniformity and discretion in Minnesota, a flagship guidelines jurisdiction.

Judging Compliance under the Minnesota Guidelines

Sentencing commissions rightly recognize the need to retain some level of judicial discretion in the form of departures from the guidelines' recommended sentences. Fixed sentences and mandatory penalties were widely lamented for their impoverishment of sentencing. They failed Aristotelian justice because they prohibit different cases from being treated differently. Guidelines needed to find a balance between encouraging uniformity and retaining a safety valve of judicial discretion. And while the best efforts at judging guidelines suggest that they have probably imparted some uniformity and reduced disparities, research has not adequately examined the degree to which guidelines have (or have not) engendered interjudge uniformity.

The analysis presented here examines the degree to which judges comply with the Minnesota guidelines' presumptive prison recommendations. Table 6.1 contains the Minnesota standard sentencing guidelines grid (there are separate grids for sex and drug offenses). Minnesota makes for a compelling test case because for some commentators, Minnesota is a model guidelines jurisdiction. Its guide-

TABLE 6.1. SENTENCING GUIDELINES GRID

Severity Level of Conviction Offense (Example offenses listed in italics)		0	1	2	3	4	5	6 or more
Murder, 2nd Degree (Intentional; Drive-By-Shootings)	11	306 *261–367*	326 *278–391*	346 *295–415*	366 *312–439*	386 *329–463*	406 *346–480*	426 *363–480*
Murder, 2nd Degree (Unintentional) Murder, 3rd Degree (Depraved Mind)	10	150 *128–180*	165 *141–198*	180 *153–216*	195 *166–234*	210 *179–252*	225 *192–270*	240 *204–288*
Murder, 3rd Degree (Drugs) Assault, 1st Degree (Great Bodily Harm)	9	86 *74–103*	98 *84–117*	110 *94–132*	122 *104–146*	134 *114–160*	146 *125–175*	158 *135–189*
Agg. Robbery, 1st Degree Burglary, 1st Degree (w/ Weapon or Assault)	8	48 *41–57*	58 *50–69*	68 *58–81*	78 *67–93*	88 *75–105*	98 *84–117*	108 *92–129*
Felony DWI Financial Exploitation of a Vulnerable Adult	7	36	42	48	54 *46–64*	60 *51–72*	66 *57–79*	72 *62–84*
Assault, 2nd Degree Burglary, 1st Degree (Occupied Dwelling)	6	21	27	33	39 *34–46*	45 *39–54*	51 *44–61*	57 *49–68*
Residential Burglary; Simple Robbery	5	18	23	28	33 *29–39*	38 *33–45*	43 *37–51*	48 *41–57*
Nonresidential Burglary	4	12	15	18	21	24 *21–28*	27 *23–32*	30 *26–36*
Theft Crimes (Over $5,000)	3	12	13	15	17	19 *17–22*	21 *18–25*	23 *20–27*
Theft Crimes ($5,000 or less); Check Forgery ($251–$2,500)	2	12	12	13	15	17	19	21 *18–25*
Assault, 4th Degree; Fleeing a Peace Officer	1	12	12	12	13	15	17	19 *17–22*

Criminal History Score

Note: Presumptive sentence lengths are in months. Italicized numbers within the grid denote the discretionary range within which a court may sentence without the sentence being deemed a departure. Offenders with stayed felony sentences may be subject to local confinement.

lines are presumptively binding, have avoided the complexities that plagued the federal system, and have allowed for effective corrections system management (Frase, 2019). The rows of the matrix in Table 6.1 indicate the severity level of the conviction offense, numbered 1 through 11, with the most serious offenses populating higher rows. The columns of the grid indicate the defendant's criminal history score, with seven columns ranging from 0 to 6 or more. The cells contain numbers representing the months of sanction recommended for an offense-offender combination. Thus, for a second-degree burglary by a defendant with a criminal history score of 3, the recommended sentence would be the range indicated by the cell that lies at the intersection of severity level 6 and criminal history score 3: between 34 and 46 months in prison (with a midpoint recommendation for 39 months). (By way of contrast and emphasis, the range for second-degree burglary in nonguidelines South Carolina is 0–180 months [i.e., anything from probation up to the 15-year maximum].) One of the most notable visual features of the Minnesota grid is the dark stair-stepped disposition line that demarcates the shaded gray nonprison zone from the white presumptive prison zone. This disposition line expresses the presumptive in/out decision that has been written about in previous chapters. All the nonshaded cells indicate a recommendation of prison for the stated range in months. All the shaded cells in the bottom southwest of the grid indicate a recommendation of nonprison (i.e., probation or other noncustodial sanctions, plus up to a year in jail—but not state prison).

An important feature of nearly all guidelines systems is not pictured: guideline departures. A departure is an official mechanism that allows a judge to deviate from the sentence recommended or dictated by the guidelines. Often judges are required to state the justification for a departure, and this deviation could trigger different standards for appellate review of the sentence, though jurisdictions vary on the details of how they are implemented. In some jurisdictions guideline recommendations are merely advisory, but in Minnesota they are presumptive, or legally binding. Still, a judge may depart from the guideline sentence by stating legally valid reasons for the departure, which are subject to appellate review under a standard of substantial and compelling circumstances (Robina Institute, n.d.; Minnesota Sentencing Guidelines, 2022, section 2.D.1).

Departures can be both aggravated and mitigated—that is, judges may impose a sentence that is either harsher or more lenient than what the guidelines call for. They can also attach to either of the two major sentencing decisions addressed in this book: a judge can depart from the in/out recommendation, and a judge can depart from the length of sentence recommendation. These are referred to as dispositional and durational departures, respectively. In part because of the additional legal challenges of aggravated departures and the overly harsh upper end of sentencing generally, mitigated departures are much more frequent than aggravated departures, and one might argue that dispositional departures are much more consequential than durational departures.[1] For instance, the decision to give probation rather than prison has a qualitatively different impact on a person's life than the decision to give 20 months in prison rather than 26. For this reason, downward dispositional departures are a particularly salient focal point of sentencing guideline policy and compliance.

Importantly, there are no formal internal or external constraints on judicial departure practices—that is, judges must comply with the law related to departures, but there is no scrutiny into whether judges depart seldom or often. Sentencing commissions sometimes report overall compliance rates (or, reciprocally, departures from the guidelines) (see, e.g., Minnesota Sentencing Guidelines Commission, 2022). These give an indication of overall compliance, but pooled compliance rates do not provide any insight into the reform objective of having more uniform practices between judges. (A small body of research examines departures, mostly related to how racial disparities [which guidelines were targeting] reemerge from departure practices [Engen et al., 2003; Ulmer and Johnson, 2017].)

Findings on Minnesota Guidelines Compliance

One approach to answering these questions would be to count how frequently judges depart and to compare their departure percentages. But the types of caseloads judges have may differ, and these case attributes could account for differences in departure rates. For example, some judges may have specialized dockets with very serious felony cases; others may be in more urban areas, where defendants are more likely to have longer criminal histories; and a small number of judges may preside over diversionary courts that are particularly likely to offer favorable dispositions for participating in the required programming. Rather than simply counting the departures, a more robust approach involves constructing a conditional likelihood of departure accounting for these different case characteristics.

To examine these questions, the current analysis relied on three recent years of Minnesota Sentencing Guidelines Commission data (2014–2016; N = 49,835). To control for case and offender characteristics, the approach involved estimating judge-specific logistic regressions, which included offense severity level, criminal history score, and categorical offense type. The logistic regressions (not shown) estimated the likelihood of a downward dispositional departure for a given judge. The average marginal effect was saved for each judge as a measure of the conditional probability of a departure for that judge, controlling for case and offender type.

Figure 6.1 shows the distribution of downward departure probabilities. Recall the question being examined here: What is the probability that a judge will issue a downward departure and impose a non-

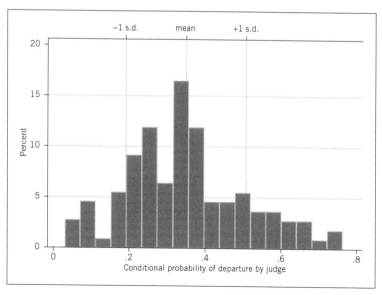

Figure 6.1 Distribution of Conditional Probabilities of Downward Dispositional Departure, by Judge

prison sentence when the guidelines call for a prison sentence? The pooled average departure probability was 35 percent, meaning that overall, judges depart in just over a third of eligible cases. However, the variation is wide. Accounting for the standard deviation, statisticians would consider departure rates between 19 percent and 51 percent to be within the typical range. Not insignificantly, there are judges who depart only 3 percent of the time, at the low extreme, and a number of judges who depart from the guidelines more than they comply with them, with departure probabilities up to 76 percent.

Importantly, these results are not mere reflections of differences in local legal cultures. In smaller counties with only a few judges, it becomes difficult to parse out whether outcomes reflect judges transmitting local culture or defining it with their personal preferences on sentencing. However, the two largest counties in Minnesota had a sufficient number of judges to analyze judge departure probabilities by county. In Hennepin (which contains the city of Minneapolis), the average downward dispositional departure probability was 36 percent, with a standard deviation range of 25–46 percent and a total range of 9–66 percent. In Ramsey (which contains the city of St. Paul), the average was 37 percent, with a standard range of 27–47 percent and a total range of 24–63 percent. Local culture no doubt influences departure practices, but the wide variation in departure decision-making cannot be written off as a mere artifact of jurisdictional differences or local legal culture. Even within a county, judges exhibit very different approaches to downward dispositional departures.

When Judge Frankel denounced American indeterminacy as "law without order" and called for the sentencing commissions that would create guidelines, the variation in sentencing across different judges (and workgroups) was precisely what he attacked. And yet almost half a century later, in what is arguably the most well-designed guidelines system in existence, this largely ignored artifact of guideline departures shows an astonishing degree of the very same phenomenon of judicial variation. Some defendants are sentenced by judges who depart twice as often as they comply with a presumptive prison sentence, while others are sentenced by judges who adhere to the guidelines over 95 percent of the time.

It is unsatisfying that we have no concrete, principled standard to establish an acceptable level of downward dispositional departures overall or with reference to the range and variation among judges. But these numbers are striking; a judge who departed from the most significant guideline pronouncement (prison or no prison) more often than he or she complied with it would be considered in the typical range of judicial compliance in this sample.

To be fair, even with this vast departure variation, sentencing under the guidelines is not entirely the law without order that Judge Frankel decried decades ago. The sentence length apportionments undoubtedly anchor prison lengths in ways that would not happen absent the guidelines. Further, even when presumptive prison recommendations are not being complied with, the guideline recommendation has some important function as it requires the judge to provide reasons for departure. Yet it does seem striking that judges departing between 20 percent and 50 percent of the time make up the typical range and that judges departing 3 percent of the time and 76 percent of the time all coexist in the same statewide sentencing scheme that is heralded as among the best of sentencing guidelines systems. Since the analyses control for offense severity level, criminal history, and offense type, these findings constitute some degree of evidence that like cases are often not treated alike under guidelines but that the personal preferences of judge and workgroup, as well as the local legal culture of a place, continue to manifest in dramatic ways.

The Tension between Uniformity and Discretion

As noted earlier in this chapter, it is not clear what the ideal compliance rate would even be. There are at least two separate inquiries, both integral to our reassessment of uniformity in sentencing. First, what is an ideal overall compliance rate? Second, how much variation by judge is acceptable? For example, if it were determined that an overall departure rate of 25 percent was desirable, then what would be an acceptable variation and range, which would also be critical? After all, a departure rate of 25 percent could be attained under such different scenarios as (1) when every judge departed in 25 percent of cases or (2) when half of all judges never departed and the other half departed in 50 percent of cases.

As a starting point for the overall rate, scientific notions of "average," "typical," and "atypical" could be instructive. The well-known concept of the bell-shaped curve describes how phenomena that comport to a "normal distribution" take on the shape of a bell curve. Innumerable examples of normal distributions and bell curves exist, from sizes of trees to grains of sand, measures of intelligence, and so on (Ellenberg, 2021). Presumably, criminal case profiles could also take on the form of a bell curve in terms of how typical or atypical they are, in the direction of either more egregious than average or less egregious than average (i.e., aggravated or mitigated cases). Scientific conventions define cases in a normal distribution as centered on the average (mean) value and consider anything within the middle 68 percent of values (34 percent of values above the mean and 34 percent of values below the mean—these are known as the standard deviation) to be "typical" even if divergent from the mean. Thus, if the average adult male height is 5 feet, 10 inches, with a standard deviation of 4 inches, a man who was 6 feet, 1 inch would be taller than average but not atypically tall. Since 68 percent of cases make up the typical range, the remaining 32 percent are considered atypical (more than one standard deviation above or below the mean), with 16 percent being high and 16 percent low. Under the example, a man would only be considered atypically tall if beyond the standard deviation range—i.e., over 6 feet, 2 inches tall.

From the concept of the normal distribution, we might have expected that judges should find about 68 percent, or two-thirds, of their cases to be "typical" and that the guidelines were designed to account for typical cases, so around 68 percent of sentences should fall within compliance. This would lead to an expectation that judges would find about 16 percent of cases to be atypically egregious and another 16 percent to be atypically mitigated. It is quite likely that cases and defendants do follow a normal distribution, but the notion of anchoring departure expectations to this paradigm breaks down for several reasons.

First, although the overall downward dispositional departure compliance rate in Minnesota is close to the typical range of the bell curve (65 percent and 68 percent, respectively), departures are asymmetrically mitigated. Upward dispositional departures—where the guidelines recommend a nonprison sentence but a judge imposes prison (presumably because of aggravating factors) are rare—less than 4 percent of cases in this sample. Part of this likely involves additional rights to appeal and stricter standards of review for aggravated departures. If prosecutors agree to a downward departure (or at least acquiesce or stand silent), the defendant will not complain about the leniency, but they would likely appeal an aggravated sentence. In addition, many observers would argue that sentences are too harsh to begin with, driven by decades of tough-on-crime politics. If the starting point for sentencing is set high, either to account for the potential worse-case scenario or to allow prosecutors a bigger bargaining chip to induce a plea deal, then more cases would be expected in the mitigated direction. The distribution of appropriate sentences thus is not normal (bell shaped) but skewed. Since there is no obvious way to account for things like the economics of plea bargaining and any level of punitive excess inherent in the guidelines, the normal distribution paradigm cannot be relied on as applied to criminal case distributions.

Furthermore, it is not just variation in criminal cases that drives departures but also variation in judicial attitudes and preferences. Judges may populate along various continua including (1) overall punitiveness and (2) commitment to guidelines compliance. If some judges are more punitive, they may be less likely to grant downward departures because they prefer the stricter default penalty recommended by the guidelines, while more lenient judges may be open to downward departures because they impart more lenient substantive justice. Separate from punitiveness, it is also possible that judges are driven by other motivations, such as a belief in the idea of the administrative commission's legitimacy to set penalties or else a contrasting resistance to such administrative rulemaking as an encroachment on judicial discretion. Consequently, there could be all sorts of complicated cross motivations, such as a more lenient judge who would prefer more lenient sentences but who at the same time holds a high view of administrative rulemaking and values adherence to commission rules as an end in itself. What is really needed is a careful qualitative analysis of the motivations and influences of departure practices, which could result in some typology of judges based on the driving factors.

Thus, even if a normal case distribution existed and we could expect an overall departure rate of around 32 percent, it would not be clear how much judges should be allowed to vary around that average. One consideration would be differences in case types, but there might also be a recognition that jurisprudential perspectives will vary among judges and that some degree of inherent difference in human judgment is acceptable. We may want judges to be somewhat similar, and at least not wildly divergent, in their punishment practices, but it is doubtful we would expect them to be identical. Presumably, if some judges departed, say, 35 percent of the time and others only 29 percent of the time, the citizenry would accept a degree of nonuniformity. The alternative notion of a departure quota would be contrived and overly rigid.

Aside from recognizing that a perfectly uniform departure rate is unrealistic, it is difficult to articulate a defensible acceptable range of departure variation, apart from some intuitive appeal to common numbers (maybe 10 percent, 20 percent, 25 percent, and 33 percent all seem like plausible candidates). As an upper limit, the notion of guidelines is stood on its head when departure rates are greater than compliance rates, so the number surely must be less than 50 percent. Then again, if punishment recommendations in the era of mass incarceration are excessive and prosecutors have an asymmetrical ability to overcharge, then one might find that an abundance of downward departures restores balance and fairness. Despite the seemingly poor fit of the bell curve in this context, one might still argue that at least 16 percent of cases are likely to be atypically mitigated and worthy of consideration of a mitigated sentence, so perhaps a minimum of a 16 percent departure rate sets a floor-level expectation for downward dispositional departure. On the other hand, one could see a principled approach in which a judge considered the even application of the law a paramount goal and sought to have the guidelines apply uniformly in his or her cases, with departures only granted in extreme cases.

Perhaps locating a target departure rate and acceptable range are simply problems with only political solutions. Sentencing commissions, appellate courts, legislatures, or the voting public could consider what they believe to be a reasonable range of departure probabilities and employ ways to persuade or coerce compliance. Observers who give preference to democratization and accountability over competing values like judicial independence might like to see published compliance rates by judge, though one could see how such scrutiny could quickly become subject to yellow journalism and a counterproductive politicization of punishment. As an alternative, it is possible that if commissions and judges began paying attention to this understudied phenomenon, some more cohesive compliance norms could develop informally. Because judges enjoy so much autonomy, there are few checks against their power, so there are few mechanisms to compel greater compliance. The primary options seem to be threats to reappointment (political pressure and media coverage) and the threat of appellate reversal, which many judges consider. A more engaged appellate review of sentencing could be a salient mechanism, but U.S. courts have mostly maintained considerable deference on sentencing discretion.

For now, the point of this analysis is that guidelines in and of themselves are not necessarily a panacea for sentencing uniformity. Considerable judicial variation in imprisonment for defendants with similar case profiles exists, so commissions may need to look for mechanisms outside the sentencing grid to increase uniformity.

Broader Lessons from South Carolina

As I will discuss in the final chapter, I am a proponent of guidelines and believe they are beneficial for a number of reasons. However, on this most important issue of homogenizing interjudge imprisonment decisions, the evidence presented in the previous section from one of the premier guidelines states suggests that additional efforts are needed to better realize the Aristotelian ideal of like cases being treated alike and different cases differently. More work toward uniformity is needed, which sets an important backdrop for why jurisdictions might care about the findings of uniformity in South Carolina. The chapter now turns to how the novel findings from this case study on nonguidelines sentencing could inform efforts in other jurisdictions.

Neoinstitutional Theory Insights

Though no clear rules emerge on the questions of ideal levels of guideline compliance, the lessons from South Carolina could hold promise for refining the balance between uniformity and discretion, even in guidelines states. This section introduces neoinstitutional theory as a framework for considering how both compulsive mechanisms like sentencing guidelines and some of the mechanisms found to influence uniformity in South Carolina could work together to achieve uniformity while retaining judicial discretion to individualize punishment.

Building on classical institutional theory, which dates back to the 1800s (Scott, 2013), neoinstitutionalism emerged as a sociological theory in the 1970s with a focus on how institutions operate in their broader environment. As Ulmer (2019) argues, courts can be seen through the neoinstitutional lens as an organizational field (see Chapter 3). James Willis, Stephen Mastrofski, and David Weisburd (2007, p. 151) similarly have noted that public service organizations are well suited for a neoinstitutional framework because these organizations "are not well-developed technically: their products or services are not well-specified, methods for their production are not well known, and competition is weak or non-existent."

Quintessential to understanding cultural effects are the neoinstitutionalism concepts of legitimacy and isomorphism. Striving for legitimacy is the neoinstitutional corollary of seeking profit in a business market field; organizations respond to the need to be seen as legitimate. As a part of this legitimacy-seeking paradigm, organizations within a field become similar to one another through a process of isomorphism. As established in the foundational work of Paul DiMaggio and Walter Powell (1983), neoinstitutionalism assumes that there is an "inexorable push towards homogenization" (p. 148) among organizations that stems from the striving for "political power and institutional legitimacy, for social as well as economic fitness" (p. 150). The basic idea is that if one organization achieves legitimacy, others will become like the successful organization to achieve the shared goal.

DiMaggio and Powell (1983) articulate three mechanisms of isomorphic change: coercive, mimetic, and normative isomorphism (see also Ulmer, 2019). Coercive isomorphism involves formal or informal force or persuasion by some influential outside organization or some cultural expectation. Normative isomorphism is associated with homogenic pressures from professional organizations, particularly through formal educational mechanisms and professional networks within the organizational field. Mimetic isomorphism refers to "copying what is constituted as culturally valuable ways of doing or arranging things—cultural capital" (Clegg, 2012, p. 167) when faced with uncertainty. Mimesis has emerged as the quintessential mechanism of isomorphism (Clegg, 2012).

The argument is this: The impositions of sentencing guidelines were attempts at coercive uniformity, and guidelines have been partially, but not entirely, successful. South Carolina displays sentencing uniformity (and legitimacy) obtained, in part, through normative and mimetic processes. Judges traveled circuits, so they interacted with professional networks across the state rather than maintaining isolation in a judicial fiefdom. And because of the circuit rotation, the opportunity to see "culturally valuable ways of doing or arranging things" flourished, encouraging mimicry as judges traveled from county to county.

Accordingly, sentencing guidelines jurisdictions (or other nonguidelines jurisdictions) could further advance their efforts toward uniformity and legitimacy by supplementing the coercive formal rules with mechanisms that foster normative and mimetic uniformity. Here I present five different potential tools that could serve as normative or mimetic vehicles.

(1) Judicial councils. Judicial councils were a short-lived preguidelines innovation that developed precisely because of internal judicial concerns over disparities.[2] As Shari Diamond and Hans Zeisel (1975) recount, councils were groups of judges who would meet regularly to discuss difficult cases. A judge could bring in a case file, and each judge would take a turn expressing what sentence they would impose. The discussions would be nonbinding on the assigned judge. As an early appraisal of a judicial council (Doyle, 1961, p. 30) put it,

> when two or more judges individually review and appraise the same presentence material on a given defendant, divergent opinions as to the sentencing considerations and dispositions frequently result. It is abundantly clear, moreover, that these same judges after discussion gained a different appreciation of the case and in two out of five instances changed their previously indicated disposition to one that conformed or approached conformity to the consensus of the group.

Diamond and Zeisel's (1975) empirical evaluation of two judicial councils found that sentencing councils reduced sentencing disparity by about 10 percent.

Judicial councils apparently fell out of favor—possibly because the earliest examples were among federal courts and may have been eclipsed by the federal Sentencing Reform Act of 1984 and the guidelines that followed. Today there is more potential for these tools than ever. In the past, councils formed in large cities where it was convenient for a critical mass of geographically close judges to meet together regularly. In the current era, geographically dispersed judges could meet together through video conferences to diversify participation.

(2) **Judicial conferences.** Judges and lawyers are typically subject to required annual continuing legal education, which they complete through attendance at workshops and conferences. Often these include talks and panels on current legal issues, case law updates, and the like. While practicing attorneys can pick and choose a daylong workshop to accommodate their schedules, it is a considerable feat to gather all a state's judges for an annual judicial conference as many states do. Time is surely in high demand at these, but an annual judicial conference does present a unique opportunity for judges to engage in norm sharing. States and the judiciary could prioritize opportunities aimed at not just providing judges with education material but also advancing other goals like uniformity and legitimacy. These could take the form of small group breakout sessions where judges discuss sentencing specifics and related issues.

(3) **Academic-practitioner workshops.** Another idea is to expand academic-practitioner sentencing workshops. Professor Dan Freed ran a workshop beginning in the 1970s in which he brought together judges and attorneys along with Yale law students to discuss cases and sentencing. A similar workshop was later run by Professor Bob Levy at the University of Minnesota Law School, and Professor Steve Chanenson has been running one through Villanova Law School for the past twenty years. In Chanenson's version, students and practitioners individually study actual case files, impose a sentence, and then come together to share their sentences and discuss why they felt that sentence was appropriate. I have participated in Professor Chanenson's workshop and have interacted with several judges across the country, including judges from South Carolina, who have participated in these workshops, and they are widely regarded as a valuable, thought-pro-

voking experience imparting insight into one's own sentencing processes.

(4) Internal compliance rate reports. This recommendation merits careful treading. It is quite likely that many judges do not actually know the statistics of how often they comply and depart over the course of a year or how their compliance rates differ from those of other judges in their court community and state. Some mechanism for self-reflection (possibly in the form of an internal judicial report) would afford judges with data-driven feedback. I recognize that such data could be used for counterproductive political purposes. For example, especially in judicial election states, political opponents could use this sort of information without appropriate context to politicize judicial selection in an undesirable way. There are of course countervailing considerations of transparency and accountability, and it is possible that the best interests of all could be served with open access to all sentencing information (see Bergstrom and Mistick, 2003). There is room for legitimate debate whether such reports should be publicly available; but as a baseline, at least an internal monitoring information system would be beneficial for informing a judge of how he or she fits into the overall state norms on this crucially important issue of compliance.

(5) Small-scale rotation. Finally, it seems naive to suggest that other states adopt (or resurrect) a full-scale system of circuit rotation. Despite its benefits, rotation is burdensome for judges who have to travel. It may cause inefficiencies in case processing and could have some unintended (and gendered) consequences related to balancing career and family goals. However, it would certainly be possible to have smaller-scale rotations that could introduce some of the benefits attributable to the South Carolina findings. For example, judges from neighboring counties could rotate; this is done to some degree in North Carolina, and a number of states use an ad hoc form of visiting judge in remote counties when conflicts arise or a lone county judge is temporarily unavailable. Temporary visiting judgeships could also be arranged—for example, by having a requirement that each judge serve a short, specified amount of time every year holding court in a different county.

This list is not exhaustive; there are likely other similar mechanisms that could be put in place or leveraged to target increased uniformity and legitimacy. More important than any specific recommendation is the need for recognition that (1) lack of uniformity issues persist, even under guidelines, and (2) normative and mimetic tools can influence uniformity.

Prior Record Policies

Although not directly relevant to uniformity, a final significant takeaway for other jurisdictions from the South Carolina research lies in the criminal history findings. As discussed in previous chapters, the defendant's prior record has long been viewed as a primary determinant of sentencing—so much so that sentencing guidelines formalized the role of prior record as one of the two dimensions on the grid, cementing its importance for both the in/out and length decisions. Yet a series of studies has pointed to negative consequences that flow from robust prior record schemes, including the exacerbation of racial disparities, disruption of proportionality in sentencing, and contribution to mass incarceration through nonviolent offenders (see Frase et al., 2015; Hester, Frase, Roberts, and Mitchell, 2018). Further, scholars have labored, with surprisingly limited success, to articulate the justifications for prior record punishments (see Hester, Frase, Roberts, and Mitchell, 2018; Roberts and von Hirsch, 2010).

Because prior record is mechanically applied in guidelines jurisdictions, and since almost all research in the past 30 years has been from those jurisdictions, the significance of criminal history has been taken as granted. This made the findings from South Carolina quite provocative. Criminal history was a strong predictor of the in/out decision but had only fractional weight in predicting sentence length compared to guidelines jurisdictions. This finding led to the exploration of the role of prior record reported in Chapter 5, as well as the historical case study delving into the origins of the guidelines grid, which is also recounted in Chapter 5. There is strong evidence that the earliest guidelines pioneers unwittingly established a robust connection between prior record and sentence length that did not exist before.

Given these findings, in addition to the negative consequences, the troubled efforts at justifying prior record policies, and the varied way that policies are crafted, sentencing commissions may be well served by embarking on a comprehensive review of their prior records policies. (Pennsylvania engaged in precisely such a review, which culminated with the 8th edition of its guidelines in 2023 [see Pennsylvania Commission on Sentencing, 2023].) The evidence seems to suggest that prior record warrants a key role for in/out decisions but that the connection between history and prison term should be much more muted than it is in current practice.

All told, each jurisdiction is unique in its legal structure overlay and court cultures. No two states are alike, and any policy or initiative employed in one state will take on the shape and influence of the laws and practices of the place in which it is embedded. The goal is not to carbon copy any practice, but there are many shared objectives. These include justice, fairness, equity, transparency, and legitimacy in many manifestations. Of perennial interest are the reform-era staples of increasing uniformity and decreasing racial disparities. These studies from South Carolina do not provide all of the answers, but they may offer some solutions to advance progress in treating like cases alike and different cases differently.

7

Conclusion

Implications and Future Directions

This book encapsulates a program of research aimed at understanding sentencing in an understudied legal context. Though the research site, South Carolina, lacked sentencing guidelines, it exhibited substantial indicia of sentencing uniformity. Over the course of the studies, several characteristics emerged that could prove insightful to other jurisdictions in the continued pursuit of improving justice in punishment. To recapitulate the main takeaways from the body of work:

1. **Initial empirical findings.** Many of the initial individual-level empirical findings reported in Chapter 3 comported with general trends found in research from other jurisdictions; legal characteristics largely drove the likelihood of receiving a prison sentence and were related to the amount of prison time imposed. Racial disparities were present though moderate, considering that this was a southern, racially diverse state with no sentencing guidelines and extensive judicial discretion. The trial penalty was pronounced, meaning that defendants insisting on a trial were much more likely to be incarcerated and were incarcerated for much

longer, on average, than similarly situated defendants who pleaded guilty. A key finding was that while a defendant's prior record was a strong predictor of whether they would be incarcerated, criminal history had little effect on the length of the sentence. This finding offered a stark contrast to sentencing guidelines policies, which place great weight on punishment length premiums based on prior record.

2. **Judge- and county-level findings.** Despite the theoretical expectations established by the courts as communities and inhabited institutions theories, there were few judge or county influences detected. The expectations for judge- and county-level variation were especially high given the lack of unifying guidelines, making the null findings all the more noteworthy. There was minimal variation in outcomes attributable to the judge and county level, and none of the judge- or county-level characteristics that were examined predicted the sentencing outcomes. These puzzling findings led to a new phase of research that relied on judge interviews to better explain these features of South Carolina court communities.

3. **Judicial rotation and plea judges.** Exploration through qualitative interviews revealed the importance of the practice of judicial rotation (South Carolina judges rotate through the different circuit courts, presiding over cases in many different counties throughout the year) and the emergence of "plea judges." Because a number of different judges rotate through a given county every year, defendants could strategically choose more favorable judges to enter pleas in front of. The term "plea judge" refers to a small number of the most lenient judges in the state who were sought out by defendants and defense attorneys. The plea judge norms had spillover effects: Since other judges knew that defendants could wait to get a better deal in front of a plea judge, they pragmatically adjusted sentences down to plea judge levels to keep dockets moving efficiently. Not all judges did this, however; some resistant "hanging judges" remained, and they often ended up presiding over trials, where the favorable enticements of plea deals played no role.

4. **Judicial rotation and statewide norms.** It was not only the plea judge effects that led to the statewide sentencing culture. Other features of the South Carolina judicial system and legal framework contributed to the uniformity. Since judges traveled, they fostered statewide networks and norms, taking ideas and practices across the counties they worked in.
5. **Judges on criminal history.** The quantitative criminal history findings were also supplemented with qualitative interview data related to the usefulness of a defendant's prior record. These data—both the quantitative analyses of the administrative sentencing data and the subsequent qualitative interviews with the judges—indicated two distinct operations of prior record. It was a strong signal for the in/out determinations, where judges must decide whether the offender can be granted a noncustodial sentence or needs a dose of incarceration. However, for the sentence length determination, prior record had minimal influence. This is in stark contrast to sentencing guidelines, where robust sentence length increases are mechanically tied to prior record. This means that guidelines jurisdictions likely have imposed a more punitive structure that has contributed to mass incarceration and that carries all sorts of unintended consequences. (This also led to some historical digging that ultimately helped to illuminate how the guidelines movement misguidedly injected an overreliance on prior record in sentencing that continues to affect policy and practice today.)
6. **Insights for other jurisdictions.** Chapter 6 presented original research and new findings raising concerns over a lack of sentencing uniformity even in one of the United States' most successful sentencing guidelines jurisdictions, Minnesota. After making the case for why all jurisdictions, including those with guidelines, should continue striving for uniformity, Chapter 6 drew on neoinstitutional theory to suggest ways other sentencing systems could apply some of the lessons from South Carolina to reach sentencing goals.

Overall, this research contributes to the literature by answering calls for studies in underexamined legal frameworks, using a mixed-methods approach that combined quantitative administrative data with qualitative interviews.

Strengths and Limitations of the Research

Two strengths of this program of research have been (1) the novelty of the nonguidelines data and (2) the mixed-methods approach that supplemented the more typical quantitative regression-based analyses with the qualitative interviews of judges. It was serendipity that I pursued my Ph.D. at the University of South Carolina, located in what is probably one of the only nonguidelines states to have collected statewide sentencing data.[1]

Empirical research should shed light on meaningful questions and that researchers should seek to advance a field of research by addressing gaps in knowledge. There are still gaps in our knowledge of courts and sentencing. Many states have never been the site of a sentencing study. Yet each state has its own unique profile of sentencing laws and local culture. Each state has a sentencing story to tell, and untold insights may be awaiting discovery. In the modern era of computer technology and data collection systems, it is disappointing that complete statewide sentencing data is not readily available, down to a person, in every jurisdiction. The stakes of punishment and the need for transparency are too great; the field needs a catalyst for progress toward complete universal data on sentencing. As the current study demonstrates, efforts to investigate substantial gaps in knowledge can provide significant returns.

A second major strength of this project was in its mixed-methods approach. Decades ago, pioneers like Malcolm Feeley (1979) and James Eisenstein and colleagues (1988) defined the field with ethnographic research. Contemporaries like John Kramer, Jeff Ulmer, Mona Lynch, and Ronald Wright and colleagues[2] have continued to produce important qualitative insights, but as a whole, quantitative studies based on administrative data have come to dominate the discipline. Scholars have issued calls for more qualitative work for decades (e.g., Blumstein et al., 1983; Lynch, 2019; Ulmer, 2012). The qualitative work reported in Chapters 4 and 5 yielded the most interesting and instructive aspects of this project. To be fair, though, it was in the context of the program of research as a whole that the qualitative findings delivered their greatest insights: The findings related to plea judges, statewide norms, and the role of prior record are meaningful because they provided rich and deep answers to questions that arose from the quantitative findings.

Of course, this study has limitations. There are a number of additional data points that ideally would be available. These include information on employment status and dependents, the defendant's detainment or lack thereof prior to case disposition, type of defense counsel, and victim information. In addition, this data only covered sentencing decisions; it did not include upstream decision-making related to case dismissals and charge reductions. These prosecutorial decisions are critically important and woefully underexamined. The full picture of case processing is crucial for a true understanding of justice, fairness, and racial equity.

Along these lines, while the qualitative judge interviews place a distinctive stamp on the current research, interviews of prosecutors, defense attorneys, and other court-adjacent actors would undoubtedly prove enlightening. Access to prosecutors has traditionally been seen as more difficult to obtain, but several recent (and not-so-recent) studies demonstrate both the possibility and benefits of prosecutorial research.

Ron Wright and Kay Levine (2014), for example, have used prosecutor interviews to explore the "young prosecutors' syndrome"—the tendency for early-career prosecutors to be overly zealous and concerned with forging their own reputations. Besiki Kutateladze, R. R. Dunlea, and colleagues have created a growing Prosecutorial Performance Indicators project, which has spawned insightful research. Richardson [Dunlea] and Kutateladze (2021) explored line prosecutor priorities in jurisdictions with newly elected, reform-minded chief prosecutors. They found that assistant prosecutors were mindful of new office priorities yet experienced some "organizational inertia" and resistance to change characteristic of many criminal justice reform contexts. Dunlea (2022) drew on prosecutor interviews to elucidate cultural scripts of color blindness and prosecutor struggles to acknowledge and address racial disparities in the criminal justice system.

Prosecutors clearly play an important role in sentencing and related decisions—Wright (2017) calls them the most important actors in criminal justice (see also Corda and Hester, 2021). Hopefully the new wave of prosecutorial research—both in terms of quantitative data access and qualitative interviews—will continue to expand.

Better Data, Better Research

Finally, there is a real need for more and better data and research—specifically, (1) data from earlier stages of the justice process, such as prosecutorial charging and dismissal decisions; (2) data from the full breadth of state jurisdictions; and (3) data that better captures the circumstances of the defendant and case, including fuller background characteristics of the defendant and victims. As Megan Kurlychek and Brian Johnson (2019) explain, there is an abundance of theoretical accumulation illustrating the ways that cumulative disadvantages accrue in the criminal justice system. Yet there is a dearth of research carefully examining cumulative impacts, largely because the data is hard to come by or difficult to link across agencies (but for counter-examples, see Kutateladze, Andiloro, Johnson, and Spohn, 2014; Rehavi and Starr, 2014). This is especially true of prosecutorial charge and dismissal decisions, which Kurlychek and Johnson (2019, p. 300) call "one of the most important and least understood stages." In addition, having more complete information on bail and pretrial detention is essential (Baughman 2019; Mayson, 2019). The evidence that does exist yields mixed and complex findings with regard to racial disparities, meaning that there are likely complex and countervailing factors and a rich milieu of processes to explain.

Prosecutors may have sound legal reasons for not wanting to divulge information related to some investigations and decisions. However, there is a baseline of information that the public is entitled to. As a general rule, data should be publicly available so one can examine every arrest charge filed, trace that charge to its conclusion, and find out whether it was dismissed or advanced and whether the charges and counts were adjusted (e.g., reduced). At a minimum, the age, race, ethnicity, and gender of the person arrested should be known, as should their pretrial status, including details on whether bond was set, for how much, and whether and for how long the defendant was detained. For cases that advance to arraignment and disposition, the data should allow researchers to link all related charges, including any dropped or reduced, to go along with standard sentencing data (standard when it is available at all, that is) on the nature and severity of the offense, prior record, and other factors.

A full wish list would include many other data points on things like type of counsel, employment history, and information about victims. There is room for debate on how extensive data should be and whether the public has access to personal identifying information. For now, I am calling instead for the data that in my view governments can no longer fail to provide. The interests of justice and fairness are too formidable, and costs of data collection and dissemination too incidental, for governments to fail to facilitate access to a transparent accounting of a fundamental aspect of a public function. Without this more complete access to key data, research on sentencing will only be illuminating pieces of the fuller story. If we are serious about the importance of justice, equity, and fairness, we have to be serious about facilitating access to data.

Future Directions: Guidelines Revisited

Despite the central thrust of this volume—that considerable uniformity in sentencing can be achieved without guidelines—there are clear benefits of sentencing guidelines, and arguably all jurisdictions should have a permanent sentencing commission and sentencing guidelines. As the analysis of Minnesota data in Chapter 6 showed, guidelines are not a panacea for uniformity, and as discussions throughout this volume related to prior records point out, there are aspects of guidelines that have been detrimental to sound sentencing policy. Despite leaving room for improvement, a guidelines commissions offer substantial advancements, including serving as punishment policy specialists, acting as a data clearinghouse, and fostering uniformity.

First, entrusting a sentencing commission (and its guidelines) with direction over punishment allows for specialized policy expertise and can help remove sentencing issues from some politicization (see, e.g., Weisberg, 2012). Commissions can be nimbler and more responsive to emerging issues. They develop expertise, drawing from an informed and diverse body of members that typically includes representatives from key stakeholder groups, such as prosecutors, defense attorneys, the judiciary, and lawmakers. Commissions are also better positioned than legislatures to connect policy initiatives across criminal justice agencies, such as through "linking sentencing policy to correctional resources to address crowding and budgetary concerns" (Weisberg, 2012, p. 39).

Second, commissions and guidelines facilitate the collection of data. Sentencing is a public function of the government that, as emphasized throughout this volume, has tremendous effects over individuals and communities. The lack of uniform and complete data is a problem, but a solvable one. Every courthouse has some type of case management system; what is needed is a statewide clearinghouse to gather annual case data and standardize it. Commissions have proved highly successful in deploying sentencing information systems and collecting annual data, and a permanent sentencing commission is probably the surest and fastest way to data.

Third, despite the analysis in Chapter 6 calling into question the downward dispositional departure variation in guidelines jurisdictions, structured sentencing makes significant strides toward uniformity while maintaining discretion. It is difficult to gauge the impact of guidelines because most guidelines are now decades old and studies are generally not able to account for historical trends, other policy implementations, or external confounders like prosecutorial adjustments to guidelines policies (see Engen, 2009; Hester, 2021). Still, there is evidence that guidelines may help reduce disparities over time and that they may help control prison populations without causing an increase in crime (R. King and Light, 2019; Reitz, 2005; Stemen et al., 2005; Stolzenberg and D'Alessio, 1994).

Making proclamations about guideline effectiveness is also difficult because researchers lack a counterfactual to compare against (the data from this volume being the rare exception, and one with limited utility given the structural and cultural aspects uncovered here). However, it seems that guidelines almost certainly help impart uniformity through the ranking of offense severity and the schemes for apportioning sentence length ranges. Further, when judges do depart from the guidelines, the fact that there is a standard policy to depart from increases the likelihood of procedural justice: At least defendants would know what punishment was recommended, and usually judges have to provide reasons for the departure, which would inform the defendant why the judge believed his or her case merited different treatment. Overall, sentencing is more transparent and discretion more guided, even if room for improvement remains.

As alluded to in Chapter 6, it is not clear how best to strike the balance between too much and too little discretion. It is quite possible that a system that, like Minnesota, demonstrates a range in conditional probabilities of downward dispositional departures from 3 percent to 76 percent (with a standard range of 20 percent to 51 percent) exhibits too little uniformity on this one key decision. On the other hand, too much restriction on discretion is also problematic. Some balance between uniformity and discretion is necessary. And while it is not clear how commissions might strike that proper balance, the existence of a commission and guidelines makes it much more likely that a system could monitor practices and make adjustments.

Perhaps commissions could do more to examine interjudge and intercounty compliance issues. Commissions could use a variety of tools to advance uniformity and legitimacy, as discussed in Chapter 6. These include not only the coercive tools of changing the guideline rules and perhaps finding enforcement mechanisms but also the normative and mimetic tools for encouraging consistency in sentencing.

States that do not have guidelines should adopt guidelines, even if only advisory descriptive guidelines. There are strong arguments to be made for a system of presumptive guidelines (see Frase, 2013). But even a baseline system of advisory descriptive guidelines would provide benefits of transparency, legitimacy, and data collection and analysis to make it worth the effort. As Robert Weisberg has asserted (2007, p. 179), a contemporary consensus has emerged that "the best possible sentencing scheme is a moderately flexible set of guidelines issued by a commission." For whatever reason, the guidelines movement in the United States has flittered out, though a non-U.S. grid style of guidelines has been spreading throughout other nations, including in England and Wales, Scotland, South Korea, Jamaica, Kenya, the Republic of North Macedonia, Nigeria, Uganda, and several Gulf states (Roberts, 2019, 2020). There is also hope that the American Law Institute's *Model Penal Code: Sentencing* might rekindle some interest in guidelines in the United States, as sentencing guidelines and a permanent sentencing commission are central to its model system (Hester, 2021).

South Carolina Sentencing Guidelines Revisited

Not only did the South Carolina research provide lessons for how other states could make strides toward uniformity and legitimacy but the judge interviews also touched on aspects of the failed guidelines effort and may provide some insight for navigating judicial opposition to guidelines reform in South Carolina and elsewhere. In fact, one judge surmised that a guidelines effort would be more successful today.

The judges I interviewed expressed a consensus that guidelines failed because of judicial opposition, which was primarily about retaining the discretion to exercise independent judgment. The vast majority of judges indicated that they had opposed the guidelines as an unwanted constraint on judicial discretion. "Judges had enough influence to kill it [the guidelines proposal]," offered Judge Adams. Judge Earle agreed, saying, "Most judges were dead set against them," although he himself was more ambiguous: "On my side of the bench, I like the freedom. But I can imagine being on the other side of the bench and feeling different." Several judges stressed a view that the legislature had elected them to exercise their independent judgment. For example, Judge Davis indicated that "judges in general didn't like them; they believed they were elected to use their own independent intellect, sense of justice, etc." Judge Isbell echoed, "The legislature elected me to sentence people. . . . I didn't want a grid that some commission came up with." "Judges need latitude and discretion," Judge Cline agreed. "Hopefully you select good judges."

Other major objections included views that the guidelines went against prevailing sentencing culture and would be circumvented. Several judges seemed to resent the guidelines as an outside effort to impose upon judicial standards. Judge Earle said, "The further away you are, the less results you get. The guidelines were an attempt to legislate from on high." Judge Hendrix elaborated:

> I think with the culture in our judicial system, one central person or committee can't broadcast out a way of doing something and get support. The criminal justice system is an enormous amalgamation of thousands of people and departments—courts, police, probation, and others—who are all making thousands of decisions on the ground every day, and that's the way

the system works. You can't just pick out one part of it from a central location and dictate things about it apart from that amalgamation and the culture of the people involved.

Judge Isbell discussed a related concern, shared by others, that prosecutorial discretion was not checked and therefore would have increased at the expense of judicial discretion. "The state retained a lot of discretion and could put a person on a part of the grid where they wanted them. They [prosecutors] just had too much discretion that way." Judge Hendrix echoed, "Nobody was going to follow them [the guidelines], and the solicitors weren't going to follow them. The solicitors could have gotten around things. There were just too many leaks and outlets, and putting restrictions on the judges but nobody else didn't make sense." According to Judge Kiley, "To a certain extent prominent criminal defense lawyers weren't in favor of them either because they thought they could get their clients a better deal without the guidelines."

Finally, several judges mentioned the influence that the experience with federal guidelines had on shaping their view of the South Carolina initiative. Judge Isbell recounted, "I'd seen how it worked in the federal courts and didn't like them. I recall one example, I forget the details now, but I think a Reagan appointee retired because they had to sentence a woman who was a drug mule to something while her husband who was the real bad guy got off with less. It just wasn't justice, and I was influenced by that." Judge Louris (who was staunchly opposed to guidelines and indicated "I hope they never resurface") said, "I talked to my friends in the federal system who spoke negatively of them," which made up part of his resistance. As evidence that South Carolina was better off for not adopting guidelines, Judge Davis brought up a story of a mayor and a governor who had committed similar crimes and received "very different sentences under the federal guidelines."

There were some judges who favored guidelines, however. Judge Farrar indicated that he supported the guidelines "because they would have resulted in more uniform sentencing and it also would have helped me to have a range." Judge Mayer appreciated the way in which they shrank the large window of sentencing options and gave the judge a narrower range to work within. Judge Andrews did not express an opinion in favor of or against guidelines but did offer an interesting opinion about judges' receptiveness to the guidelines. He noted that judges had been adamantly opposed to the guidelines around 2000 and explained the cause as "robe-itis," which he defined thus: "Every judge had the view that every other judge should do what *they* were doing with sentencing." Judge Kiley, a proponent of guidelines, made a similar comment: "Every judge has their own set of sentencing guidelines, and they all think they're right, but they're all different. There's huge disparity, and there shouldn't be." Judge Mayer noted that he was particularly in favor of guidelines in South Carolina, where judges typically do not have the benefit of presentence investigation reports. Overall, he saw room for balance between following the guidelines and using judgment: "I think they are good as long as we don't lose common sense along with the statistics." He offered a colorful diagnosis of the bench's opposition to guidelines: "Part of it is judges being like boys on the playground having a pissing contest over not taking their discretion away."

Finally, several judges indicated some ambivalence. Judge Bennett, who thought guidelines would be too time consuming, showed a clear understanding of both advisory and presumptive guidelines, noting that he had not otherwise had negative feelings toward the guidelines proposal because they were advisory and because "even with some mandatory guidelines, judges can exercise discretion to depart from the guidelines." Judge Bennett also noted that if the South Carolina initiative had gone further, "I would have wanted to ensure similar safeguards to maintain some degree of judicial discretion was maintained." Judge Earle preferred the flexibility of discretion on his side of the bench but could see the appeal from the defendant's perspective. Even Judge Hendrix, who gave a condemning account of how guidelines went against the culture of the system, mused, "I kinda like the idea, but nobody was going to follow them." Judge Isbell, the staunch opponent, was also reflective: "I may have been wrong . . . now I can see some appeal in consistency being important, but I don't know, one size just doesn't fit all. I'm not sure you can say we need to serve everybody from the same spoon. Some people are really truly remorseful; some have made few mistakes; others not." Finally, Judge Adams suggested that the new generation of judges might be less resistant to guidelines: "Now judges have changed. Today judges would be much more receptive to guidelines and things like drug courts."

Whether judges in South Carolina and other jurisdictions would now be more open to the incorporation of guidelines, as Judge Adams suggested, remains to be seen. The issue of discretion emerged as a primary reason for opposing guidelines. However, the concerns over discretion did not necessarily reflect the operation of successful guidelines states (and the *Model Penal Code: Sentencing*'s system), which maintain considerable levels of judicial discretion. In fact, as argued in Chapter 6, even presumptive guidelines may well embody the retention of too much judicial discretion at the expense of uniformity. Ultimately, guidelines seem to offer an improvement with their support for Aristotelian notions of justice and other objectives, such as making data available so that scholars and practitioners can examine practices and continue to strive for justice.

Sentencing and punishment in the United States is at an interesting stage. The decade between 2010 and 2020 marked the first time in half a century that the U.S. prison population ceased to grow precipitously. Perhaps the United States reached the peak of mass incarceration; meaningful declines have certainly occurred in many states, though incarceration rates continue to grow or hold steady in some jurisdictions. The atmosphere around race and justice was also heightened in the last half of the 2010s, and the phenomenon of progressive prosecutors emerged around that time. Yet overall sentencing reform policy has found itself in a state of entropy. Throughout the 1980s and 1990s, a flurry of significant and far-reaching punishment reforms revolutionized sentencing structures in some states—these reforms included the adoption of guidelines, abolition of parole, and implementation of punitive policies such as three strikes, TIS, and mandatory minimums. Since then, nonguidelines states have appeared to lose interest in the concept of sentencing guidelines.

Thus we find ourselves in a context of heightened interest in justice and fairness but have no cohesive direction for sentencing reform. Jurisdictions are deeply dualistic, with some places having an ample supply of structured sentencing and data and others a dearth. Many states have fully embraced sentencing guidelines and commissions and have the administrative data to monitor case processing, projections, and metrics of fairness. But even more states have no guidelines, no permanent commission, and no way to examine their practices.

Whatever its shortcomings and omissions, I hope this volume illustrates that, with data, scholars and practitioners can evaluate sentencing outcomes and gather information. Every jurisdiction has a story, and if we are willing to look, we may find insights for moving sentencing policy a little closer to the Aristotelian ideal—treating like cases alike and different cases differently by engendering uniformity while retaining sufficient discretion for individualizing justice.

Methodological Appendix

Data, Methodologies, and Analytic Strategies

To maximize the readability while maintaining academic rigor, this Methodological Appendix contains supplemental information on data collection and analysis and on statistical modeling approaches.

Chapter 3: Individual-Level Models

Data

The defendant-level data consist of criminal cases sentenced in South Carolina circuit courts (the courts of general jurisdiction) for the fiscal year 2001, which were originally compiled by the now-defunct South Carolina Sentencing Commission. The circuit courts have jurisdiction over felony and serious misdemeanor offenses.[1] The analysis includes all felony cases, as well as cases that South Carolina labeled misdemeanors but that might be labeled felonies in other jurisdictions. For instance, several South Carolina misdemeanors carried maximum penalties of several years in prison, with some carrying up to 10 years in prison. During fiscal year 2001, aggravated assault, obviously a serious crime and one of the most common offenses in the data, was labeled by South Carolina law as an unclassified misdemeanor with a maximum penalty of 10 years in prison. Excluding such serious offenses solely because of the designation as misdemeanor rather than felony seemed inappropriate. Accordingly, all misdemeanors that met the traditional definition of a felony—that is, those subject to a custody sentence of more than one year in prison—were included.[2]

The original commission data did not include whether offenders pleaded guilty or were sentenced after a trial. Because prior research has found mode of disposition to be a significant predictor of both the incarceration and sentence length decisions (Kramer and Ulmer, 2009; Spohn, 2009), I supplemented the commission data with the mode of disposition through a request to the South Carolina Court Administration.[3] The data also included 429 individuals who were sentenced twice in fiscal year 2001 and constituted two separate cases. In these instances, only the most serious offense entry was kept. The commission data did not distinguish Hispanic offenders and apparently accounted for nonwhite and non-Black offenders inconsistently. Thus, we dropped 221 individuals whose race was entered as "other." Four cases were deleted for missing data on offense seriousness, and two were dropped for missing offender race. Finally, 28 offenders had missing values for their prison sentence. These delimitations resulted in a dataset of 17,643 offender cases, including 6,611 offenders who were incarcerated (i.e., sentenced to a prison term greater than 0). These cases represented all offenders convicted of a felony (or serious misdemeanor carrying a maximum of a year or more in prison) who were sentenced by active circuit judges in the general jurisdiction courts for fiscal year 2001.

Measures

A brief description of the measures is provided in Chapter 3. The primary dependent variable, *prison term*, is an offender's expected minimum sentence[4] (Freiburger and Hilinski, 2013; see also Chiricos and Bales, 1991; Spohn and Cederblom, 1991) rounded to the nearest month.[5] Because the data include extreme outliers such as life and death sentences, sentences were top coded at 470 months, or an expected minimum sentence of just over 39 years in prison. The *offense seriousness* measure was an ordinal measure of the severity of a crime based on the South Carolina Crime Classification Scheme. Offenses were coded 1 for misdemeanors carrying a possible sentence of over a year in prison, 2 for Class F felonies, 3 for Class E felonies, 4 for Class D felonies, and 5 for Class A, B, or C felonies (or unclassified felonies). The South Carolina Sentencing Commission also created a measure of an offender's *criminal history*, for which four points were assigned for each prior violent or drug-trafficking conviction with a sentence of a year or greater, two points for prior sentences of less than a year, and one point (up to a maximum of five) for prior nonincarceration convictions. Offenders with a score of 0 were deemed to have had no prior criminal history, while those with 1–3 had minimal, 4–12 had moderate, 13–20 had considerable, and 21 and over had extensive criminal histories.

Commitment score was an ordinal count based on the number and severity of the offenses for which one was currently found guilty. All offenders received one point for their main offense. Beyond that, offenders were given one point for each additional count or offense unless any of those additional offenses were for an A, B, C, or exempt felony offense; in these instances, four points were added to the commitment score. The points were then summed to create the multiple offense score (top coded at 12). (Note that the commitment score was constructed post hoc by the commission and thus was not available to or considered by the sentencing judge. It is included as a proxy to measure the nature and number of offenses for those offenders sentenced after pleading guilty or being found guilty of multiple offenses, which are not otherwise accounted for but which likely would be considered by the sentencing judge.)

Offense type was a 10-category nominal indicator for the type of crime committed: homicide, rape, robbery, assault, burglary, drug distribution, drug possession, larceny, fraud, and other. *Trial* was a binary indicator of whether the offender was found guilty after a trial rather than entering a guilty plea. In addition, mandatory minimums can have pronounced effects on sentencing outcomes (Kautt and DeLone, 2006; Rehavi and Starr, 2014). *Mandatory minimum* was a binary indicator identifying the 34 offense codes that carried a nonsuspendible mandatory prison term.

Finally, several extralegal characteristics were included. *Black* was a dummy variable indicating whether the offender was African American or white (reference category). *Male* indicated the offender's gender (female was the reference category). *Age* was the age of the offender (in years) at the time of admission.

Analytic Strategy

The analytic approach for this chapter centered on the zero-truncated negative binomial model (ZTNB) introduced by Hester and Hartman (2017). For a full treatment of issues related to potential selection bias issues and our motivation for introducing the ZTNB, readers are referred to that article. As a brief overview, the ZTNB is a count model, which is appropriate for skewed, nonnormally distributed outcomes like sentences (i.e., most individuals get no prison, and shorter sentences are more abundant than longer ones, giving the distribution a long right-tailed skew). As Scott Long (1997, p. 217) and others note, using ordinary least squares (OLS) regression to analyze untransformed event counts is inadvisable because OLS can cause "inefficient, inconsistent, and biased estimates." As a workaround, many criminal sentencing scholars have opted to use a log-transformed measure of sentence length for those who are incarcerated (e.g., Freiburger and Hilinski, 2013; Spohn and Cederblom, 1991; Spohn and DeLone, 2000; Steffensmeier and Demuth, 2000; Steffensmeier, Ulmer, and Kramer, 1998). This common practice has arisen largely because of the unique nature of sentencing-dependent variables, most notably their highly skewed, nonnegative, and intrinsically heteroskedastic distributions (Cameron and Trivedi, 2013).

Joshua Fischman and Max Schanzenbach (2012, p.738, n20) defend this practice in the sentencing context: "OLS regression with robust standard errors still provides consistent estimates, even when the error terms are not normally distributed." Yet J. M. C. Santos Silva and Silvana Tenreyro (2006, p. 641) argue that "in the presence of heteroskedasticity, estimates obtained using log-linearized models are severely biased, distorting the interpretation of the model." They demonstrate that this bias occurs because the expected value of a log-transformed variable depends on higher-order moments of its distribution. In other words, "if the errors are heteroskedastic, the transformed errors will be generally correlated with the covariates." (Santos Silva and Tenreyro, 2006, p. 653). Joseph Hilbe (2014, p. 17) also argues that "when the count response is logged and modeled using linear regression, its predicted values are nearly always distant from the actual or observed counts," which is, of course, undesirable. Hilbe emphatically advises: "*Reject the temptation to use linear regression to model a logged count*" (p. 17, emphasis in original).

My colleague Todd Hartman and I (Hester and Hartman, 2017) explored several count models, specifying three different models—the Poisson regression model, negative binomial regression model, and the hurdle regression model using the negative binomial distribution (HRM-NB)—to determine the best fit for our sentencing data.[6] Through several formal tests of model fit and Monte Carlo simulations, we determined that OLS models generated "wildly inaccurate estimates of the true effect" and that "the models designed to account for zero-inflation and overdispersion produce trivial percentages of relative bias (<1%)." (This description of the data, method, and analytic strategy for Chapter 3 draws on material published by Hester [2012]; and Hester and Hartman [2017].)

Chapter 3: Multilevel Models

Data
The judge- and county-level models examined in Chapter 3 use the same defendant-level datasets, with judge and county measures obtained as described in the text of Chapter 3.

Analytic Strategy
The chapter employed multilevel modeling strategies—hierarchical logistic regression models[7] for the incarceration decision and hierarchical linear regression models for the sentence length decision. Multilevel modeling accounts for the nested nature of offenders sentenced by judges or within counties by correcting for the correlated error that can arise from group clustering (i.e., offenders sentenced by the same judge or within the same county are not truly independent of one another because they are sentenced by the same court actor or same court community). In addition, multilevel modeling techniques allow significance tests based on the proper degrees of freedom (Johnson, 2005, 2012; Raudenbush and Bryk, 2002; Steiner, 2009). For example, if a county-level measure such as county caseload were inserted into a standard logistic regression for the in/out decision, the significance test would be based on degrees of freedom derived from the individual-level sample size here of 17,671. However, county caseload is a county characteristic, and significance tests should be based on the county-level sample size of 46. Failure to use a multilevel strategy would artificially in-

flate the statistical power of the significance tests, increasing the likelihood of Type I errors.[8] Using a multilevel modeling strategy involved estimating several different models for each outcome. First, unconditional models were estimated for each set of analyses. Unconditional models do not contain any predictor variables; they are analogous to a one-way analysis of variance (ANOVA) and indicate how much variation in outcomes lies within and between level-2 aggregates (i.e., differences in outcomes for offenders sentenced by the same judge or in the same county and differences in outcomes for offenders across judges or counties) (Raudenbush and Bryk, 2002; Wooldredge, Griffin, and Pratt, 2001). If significant variation existed at the aggregate level, the second set of models, known as random coefficients models, were run.

Random coefficients models were populated with the level-1 predictors (offender-level measures here). They did not include any level-2 measures as predictors, but the technique adjusts for statistical dependence due to the nesting of offenders within level-2 groupings. These models were not reported for the current study. Instead, the results in Chapter 4 focus on the fully specified level-2 main effects models (also known as intercepts-as-outcomes models) (Raudenbush and Bryk, 2002). These models included the level-2 characteristics discussed in the chapter and tested whether these judge- or county-level predictors bore a statistically significant relationship with the level-2 variation in incarceration rates and sentence length while controlling for the individual-level independent variables. The individual-level variables in all populated models were grand mean centered. Grand mean centering controls for individual-level effects and provides for more rigorous tests of the level-2 effects, which were the focus of this study (Enders and Tofighi, 2007; Johnson, 2006; Raudenbush and Bryk, 2002).

As alluded to in the chapter, the number of level-2 variables that could be analyzed was limited because of the small number of level-2 aggregates—46 counties and 50 judges—that served as the baseline for determining the degrees of freedom for the level-2 tests (Raudenbush and Bryk, 2002; Wooldredge, Griffin, and Rauschenberg, 2005, pp. 844–845). This selection process was guided by the courts as communities theory as well as the analysis of bivariate correlations of the predictors and outcome measures, which were not reported (but see Hester, 2012).

I also note here that prior research from other jurisdictions examines 3-level models, in which defendants are nested within judges that are nested within counties (Johnson, 2006). This traditional 3-level modeling was not possible given the non-nested structure of judges who rotated from county to county. It is possible, however, to execute a cross-classified model that would allow for such a structure (see Hester, 2012; Johnson, 2012). These models did not provide any substantial contributions or differences of findings in my prior work with this data, so they are omitted from this analysis for the sake of space and parsimony. (Those results are available in Hester, 2012, and this discussion of analytic method also draws on Hester, 2012.)

Chapters 4 and 5: Judge Interviews

Researchers have called for more qualitative examinations of criminal courts for a number of years, in large part because qualitative methods provide the potential for depth and insight to complement quantitative findings. Ken Goldstein (2002, p. 669) notes that elite interviews[9] are beneficial for "(1) gathering information from a sample of officials in order to make generalizable claims about all such officials' characteristics or decisions; (2) discovering a particular piece of information; . . . (3) informing or guiding work that uses other sources of data." Qualitative judge studies have shed light on a number of aspects of sentencing theory. For instance, Kathleen Daly (1989) interviewed judges to probe why female offenders are sentenced more leniently than males. She found evidence of a judicial paternalism aimed at the protection of children and families rather than the women themselves, and this was true among both male and female judges. Kramer and Ulmer (2002) used qualitative interviews with judges to explore ways in which workgroups disagreed with certain policy decisions imposed by the Pennsylvania sentencing grid (for example, sentences for very high severity offenses and for offenders of low-severity offenses who have extensive prior records). Ulmer and Kramer (1996) have interviewed judges and attorneys to explore quantitative findings related to trial penalties. They found that workgroup members generally agreed that trial penalties were a way to encourage guilty pleas; that pleas were viewed as a sign of remorse; and that pleading led to a less severe penalty at least in part because it allowed the defendant to avoid "emotional reactions to 'ugly facts'" that often come out in trial (Ulmer and Kramer, 1996, p. 396). Most recently, researchers have employed judge interviews to explore different strategies trial judges use to address racial disparities in various phases of the judicial process (Clair and Winter, 2016). Along these lines, qualitative inquiry was especially appealing for the current project given the findings related to county-level variation uncovered in prior research and, more generally, given that little exists theoretically on the question of what factors and features might make a jurisdiction more likely to exhibit greater statewide legal culture.

Data

A purposive sample of 13 of the 50 trial judges who sentenced offenders in the 2001 dataset were interviewed. I chose the population of the 50 judges from 2001 judges for the sampling frame because the findings of court community uniformity had been based on the practices of those judges. Though interviewing the 2001 bench sacrificed some contemporaneity, it maximized the potential to draw theoretical inferences back to the findings of uniformity.

Unlike in quantitative analyses, where the appropriate N for a random sample can be identified on the basis of statistical power and other methodological needs, selecting the appropriate number of cases in qualitative work is more difficult to determine (see Roulston, 2010), though a significant body of literature has recently developed on this issue (see, e.g., Francis et al., 2010; Guest et al., 2006;

O'Reilly and Parker, 2013). Much of the scholarship is devoted to determining when the researcher has reached "saturation," the point at which the interviews provide a "full and complete description" (Becker, 1998) of the research question and after which further data collection would be largely redundant (Corbin and Strauss, 2008; Creswell, 2014; Guest et al., 2014; see also Jacobs and Wright, 1999).

The appropriate sample size for reaching saturation is highly variable from project to project and depends on the research question, the population being studied, and the overall design of the research. For instance, Anton Kuzel (1992) suggests that 6 to 8 interviews are appropriate for a homogenous sample, while 12 to 20 should be obtained where greater variation exists. Others offer different suggestions (for a review, see Guest et al., 2006, p. 61), but a few guiding principles emerge from the literature: (1) The researcher should begin with some expected sampling frame in mind; (2) the researcher should be flexible and continue sampling if saturation has not been reached; and (3) the researcher should have some a priori criterion for when saturation has been achieved—in other words, a stopping condition (Francis et al., 2010; Guest et al., 2006; see, e.g., Mullins et al., 2004).

I began with the assumption that given the practice of rotation and the homogeneity of the judicial profession, the number of judges needed for this project would be relatively modest. For one, judges in general go through considerable selection and professional socialization processes that tend to make them a homogenous population. Greg Guest and colleagues (2006, p. 74) suggest that samples as small as four individuals may be adequate where the subjects are specialists who "possess a certain degree of expertise about the domain of inquiry," on the basis of the idea that higher degrees of professionalism and expertise increase the homogeneity of the sampling frame. Further, in the decades leading up to 2001, there was only one law school in the state, which most of the judges on the bench at this time attended. Thus, apart from the general similarities and strong socialization processes that have frequently been noted as applying to judges (see, e.g., Crow and Gertz, 2008; Johnson, 2006; Spohn, 1990; Steffensmeier and Britt, 2001), there would have been considerable overlap in both the specific socialization processes (professors, curriculum, etc.) and the networks of these South Carolina judges.

In addition, since geographic coverage is closely tied to the issue of state culture, the county of residence was a factor for sample size consideration. On average, the 50 judges held court in 12 different counties in 2001; thus adequate coverage was almost guaranteed because of the extensiveness of rotation. The 13 judges ultimately interviewed held residency in 10 of the 16 circuits (two were "at large," and two were residents in the same county) and sentenced offenders in all but 4 of the state's 46 counties during 2001. Thus, on the particular question of the likely influence of judicial rotation, the judges provided considerable geographical coverage and would all be well suited to provide an informed perspective on county differences.

Following Kuzel's recommendations, I initially anticipated that interviewing around 8 judges who varied primarily along the punitiveness continuum would be sufficient to provide saturation. While the first 8 interviews revealed all of the statewide norm concepts ultimately identified in the final sample of 13, I expanded the interviews through theoretical sampling (see Charmaz, 2002, p. 689; see also, e.g., Mullins et al., 2004) after they revealed a mechanism for uniformity that I had not anticipated (i.e., the phenomenon of the plea judge and practices related to judge shopping and plea routing). While the plea judge concept came up in the first interview and was a feature throughout the first eight, I wanted to ensure it had adequately been explored since it had not been anticipated. This led me to seek interviews with two additional judges who sentenced among the greatest number of offenders in 2001 (as the number of offenders sentenced was a key component of the plea judge concept) and who were among the most lenient; I also added interviews with two more punitive judges because the concept of the punitive "hanging judge" emerged as an important corollary to the plea judge. Finally, I added one final judge who was near the mean on the punitiveness measure so that the final sample was not overly representative of the punitiveness extremes. These additions brought the final number of judges interviewed to 13.

Data Collection

The interviews were conducted by the author between December 2014 and March 2015. They ranged from 30 minutes to over an hour and averaged 45 minutes. Given the regional differences between the author and judges and the pressing schedules of the traveling judges, the interviews were conducted via telephone[10] (see Berry, 2002; Stephens, 2007; Holt, 2010; see also Katz, 2001). Interview methodology necessarily raises the potential for various "interactional problems," which include ethical issues and technical aspects of the interview approach (Roulston, 2014). These issues include maintaining confidentiality, disclosing the purpose of the interviews, establishing rapport, getting cooperative responses, and asking questions clearly in terms the participants can readily understand and engage with (Kvale and Brinkmann, 2009; Roulston, 2014; Silverman, 2013; Smigel, 1958). As for the ethical issues, I began each interview by introducing myself, my academic affiliation, and my background and by expressing my interest in sentencing generally and in South Carolina sentencing particularly. I informed the judges that the interviews were voluntary and that their identities would remain confidential, and I invited them to ask any questions about the research project, my interest in the subject, or anything else related to the interview request.

Interviewing elites, and court elites in particular, carries with it a special set of challenges related to access to participants and the cooperation of participants (Goldstein, 2002; Smigel, 1958). Erwin Smigel (1958) emphasizes the paramount need to create interest in the subject for the participant of a legal elite interview. In introducing the project, I explained that I was interested in studying sentencing in general and that in particular I had been studying sentencing in South Carolina for some time using the 2001 sentencing commission data. I had familiarized myself with each judge's professional background from his or her biographical profile in the 2000 and 2001 South Carolina Legislative Manuals, which are small books published by the state's legislature and which contain information about various elected public officials and the state's judges. Early in the interactions, I signaled to the judges that I was familiar with their state's legal system; for instance, I referred to South Carolina prosecutors as "solicitors" rather than "DAs," I referenced the "circuit courts," and I knew to call terms of criminal court "general sessions." My objective was not to present myself as an expert but to present myself as a researcher who was a serious student of this particular legal system so that the judges could fill in some gaps in the way sentencing worked and provide their perspective on the issues discussed. The judges appeared to be naturally interested in criminal sentencing as a subject of social importance and a significant part of their experience as trial court judges.

To establish rapport, I began with a broad, open-ended question about the judge's general approach to fashioning an appropriate sentence in a case. This question was an effective opening to the interviews; the precedent was established of the author asking a short question and the judge subsequently doing most of the talking, but with frequent probing and follow-up by the author (on the importance of short questions and long answers and probing in interview methodology, see, e.g., Bernard and Ryan, 2010, chap. 2; Roulston, 2014). The interviews were semistructured and employed mostly open-ended questions. Following are examples of some of the most pertinent questions from the interview guide for the current study:

APPROACH TO SENTENCING

For a typical case, what is your approach for identifying an appropriate sentence? What case or offender characteristics matter the most?

How influential are other parties in shaping your sentence (the prosecutor, defense attorney, the defendant, victims, etc.)?

How often do you take a straight-up plea versus a recommendation or a negotiated plea?

SOUTH CAROLINA LEGAL CULTURE

What are your thoughts on the practice of judicial rotation in South Carolina? What are the benefits and burdens?

Can you give any examples of regional or county-to-county differences in sentencing and criminal-case-processing norms that you've seen as you've held court in different parts of the state?

I informed the judges that I had previously conducted empirical studies of sentencing in South Carolina using the 2001 data collected by the former sentencing commission and that I was specifically interested in sentencing practices as they had existed at that time. To the extent that practices or norms had evolved since 2001, I asked them to frame their answers with reference to that earlier period.

The judges all recalled the previous guidelines effort, and most were aware that the commission had collected some sentencing data. To minimize researcher bias, I did not inform the judges of the empirical findings (at least not at the outset of the interviews; on several occasions the findings did come up after the interviews had been concluded). I posed the question about judicial rotation in a neutral way that did not suggest any policy linkages; I simply asked what the judge's thoughts were on the practice and what the benefits and burdens were. I also framed the more closed-ended question of county-to-county variations as one of differences (rather than, for example, asking whether the judge would agree that sentencing is mostly similar across counties). The judges were also questioned about several issues not covered in the current study, including the degree to which prior records influenced their sentencing and their thoughts on the failed sentencing guidelines effort in South Carolina. (This account draws on Hester, 2017.)

Chapter 6: Minnesota Guidelines Data Analysis

Data

For the Minnesota analysis, I used annual monitoring data maintained by the Minnesota Sentencing Guidelines Commission for the three-year period covering 2014–2016 ($N = 49,835$). As noted in the chapter, several forms of guideline departure are possible. Departures can be *dispositional* (when the defendant is given a more lenient or harsher mode of punishment than presumed under the guidelines—such as a prison sentence when jail or probation is recommended) or *durational* (when the defendant is given a shorter or longer dosage of punishment than called for by the guidelines—for example, a seven-year prison sentence when a five-year sentence is called for). Either of these types of departures can be in the direction of more punishment or less punishment—aggravated or mitigated. *Aggravated* departures deviate from the presumptive sentence by imposing a more punitive disposition or duration. Reciprocally, *mitigated* departures impart less punishment and can also be dispositional (probation or jail when prison is called for) or durational. Prior research has emphasized the importance of the incarceration (in/out) decision and the role of downward dispositional departures, where the guidelines provide a presumptive sentence of prison and the judge decides whether to impose that prison sentence or grant a mitigated departure that allows the offender to avoid prison. On this question, only presumptive prison sentences are analyzed (Engen et al., 2003). For the current data, there were 16,709 presumptive prison sentence cases, making up 34 percent of the total observations. For the period of this study, Minnesota operated under two separate sentencing grids, a standard grid and a sex offender grid (of the 49,835 cases, 3,020, or 6 percent, were sentenced under the sex offender grid[11]). The current project focused on downward dispositional departures, exclusive of sex grid cases.[12] These selections generated a universe of 14,687 cases for analysis: all defendants with a presumptive prison sentence on the standard grid during the three-year period of study.

The Minnesota Sentencing Guidelines Commission data included a number of control measures. For these sparse models, only three independent variables—guidelines severity level (1–11), criminal history score (0–6), and offense type category (violent, drug, property, and other)—were considered for developing the conditional probabilities of departure.

Analytic Strategy

As an initial measure of judicial variation in downward dispositional departure rates, judge-specific logistic regressions were estimated to obtain conditional probabilities of the likelihood of departure, controlling for the guidelines offense level and criminal history scores, as well as the four-category offense type. (Supplemental analyses also calculated the raw downward dispositional departure rates for each judge, but the analysis focuses on the conditional probabilities to account for the potential differences in caseload types across judges.) The conditional probabilities could range from 0 percent to 100 percent representing the predicted probability that a defendant sentenced by that particular judge would receive a downward dispositional departure for a selected case profile. The selected case profile specified an offense level 6, criminal history score of 3, and a person offense. Notably, some judges in the dataset may have only sentenced a handful of cases in the time period. To help ensure stable regression estimates, only judges who had sentenced at least 45 cases that were presumptive prison commits (and thus eligible for a downward dispositional departure) were included in this analysis. That restriction resulted in the conditional probability analysis including 115 judges covering 9,768 cases.

Notes

Chapter 1

1. See, e.g., Spohn and Holleran (2000), who examined data collected in Cook County, Illinois; Date County, Florida; and Jackson County, Missouri, as one example.

Chapter 2

1. The difference is a significant one for sentencing guidelines. Presumptive guidelines, like those in Minnesota, are closer to being mandatory and binding on the judge, while advisory guidelines, like those in Pennsylvania, are not binding but, as the name suggests, merely advisory.

Chapter 3

1. Lynch (2019) observes that the concept of focal concerns traces back to a 1958 publication by Walter Miller and was first imported into the field of criminology by Peter Hoffman (1972) (whose work is featured later in this book, in Chapter 5).

2. The work presented draws on previously published work, including Hester, 2012; Hester and Sevigny, 2016; Koons-Witt et al., 2014; Hester and Hartman, 2017.

3. There are minor differences in the results presented here compared to previously published findings in Hester and Hartman, 2017; Hester and Sevigny, 2016; Koons-Witt et al., 2014, which reflect differences in modeling decisions.
4. The results are generally in keeping with the large body of sentencing research that tends to find some evidence of racial disparities for the in/out decision and little or no race differences in the length decision (e.g., Baumer, 2013; Mitchell, 2005; Spohn, 2000). But see van Cleve, 2016, for evidence of substantial disparities using ethnographic methods.

Chapter 4

1. See, for example, Frazier and Bock, 1982; Gruhl et al., 1981; Johnson, 2006; Kritzer and Uhlman, 1977; Myers and Talarico, 1987; Spohn, 1990; Steffensmeier and Britt, 2001; Steffensmeier and Hebert, 1999; Welch et al., 1988; Worden, 1995.
2. Only one of the 13 judges interviewed was female. However, in 2001, only three of the state's 50 trial judges were women.
3. To ensure the confidentiality of the interviews and protect the identity of the judges, pseudonyms are used for all of the judges and for some geographic areas.
4. One judge suggested that recommendations were becoming more and more common in recent years because of the use of a standard sentencing sheet that indicated whether a recommendation had been made. According to this interviewee, many judges feel that a recommendation gives them some cover from later criticism.
5. All analyses performed with Stata. For the incarceration percentage model, $p = .003$; for the average sentence length model, $p = .056$.
6. See, for example, Baumer, 2013; Engen and Steen, 2000; Kim et al., 2015; Wright and Levine, 2014.
7. Compare, for example, Pfaff, 2006, and Tonry, 1996, 2016, with Piehl and Bushway, 2007, and Harmon, 2013.

Chapter 5

1. These consisted of Calpin et al., 1982; Gottfredson, Hoffman, et al., 1975; Gottfredson, Wilkins, and Hoffman, 1978; Wilkins et al., 1978; see also Carrow et al., 1985.
2. "The origin of the sentencing guidelines project lies in the pioneering work on parole decision making conducted by the United States Parole Commission and the [NCCD] . . . under the direction of Leslie T. Wilkins and Don M. Gottfredson" (Calpin et al., 1982, p. 2).

Chapter 6

1. For the three years of analysis presented here (2014–2016), only 3.7 percent of cases were aggravated dispositional departures and only 1.47 percent were aggravated durational departures.

2. I am grateful to Professor Steve Chanenson for bringing judicial sentencing councils to my attention.

Chapter 7

1. There have been some studies based on samples collected in nonguidelines states (e.g., Kutateladze, Andiloro, Johnson, and Spohn, 2014; Rodriguez et al., 2006; Spohn and Holleran, 2000), and the BJS State Court Processing Statistics sampled 40 of the largest 75 counties in the United States, some of which were in nonguidelines states. As far as I can find, the only other nonguidelines state to accumulate complete sentencing data for analysis has been New York (see Ridgeway et al., 2020), made possible by the 2010 establishment of the New York State Permanent Commission on Sentencing.

Credit for "discovering" the commission data goes to the industry of Professors Eric Sevigny and John Burrow (both of whom would later serve on my dissertation committee), who obtained the sentencing data and archive of associated South Carolina Sentencing Commission material.

2. Although these and other studies reflect a new wave of qualitative courts research, others, including Kramer, Ulmer, and colleagues, have supplemented quantitative research with qualitative interviews of judges, prosecutors, and defense attorneys for decades (see, e.g., Johnson et al., 2008; Kramer and Ulmer, 2002; Ulmer and Kramer, 1998).

Methodological Appendix

1. During fiscal year 2001, lower-level magistrate courts had jurisdiction to sentence offenses subject to a maximum 30 days' incarceration, a $500 fine, or both; or up to one year in prison, a $5,500 fine, or both upon transfer from the circuit court (S.C. Code §§ 22-3-550, -545). Criminal jurisdiction for all other cases rested with the circuit courts (S.C. Code § 14-25-65). The commission data did not contain a record of all misdemeanor offenders sentenced in the lower courts. Because neither the complete population nor a representative sample of misdemeanor offenders was available, it was not possible to examine the universe of misdemeanor and felony sentencing outcomes. Accordingly, we included all felonies and serious misdemeanors carrying the potential for more than one year of incarceration, which is the traditional definition of a felony offense (McAninch et al., 2007). This allowed us to include offenses that were deemed serious enough by the South Carolina legislature to merit the potential for more than a year in prison, while also removing the unrepresentative portion of misdemeanor offenses that happened to have been sentenced in circuit court rather than a lower-level court. Classifying offenses this way also makes these analyses more comparable to the existing research on felony sentencing conducted in other states, rather than constituting a study marked by anomalous state law designations.

2. While misdemeanors with potential prison sentences of more than one year were included as the lowest offense severity level, we recoded the unclassified common law offenses that were subject to 10 year maximums as Class E felonies because Class E felonies were capped at a maximum of 10 years (S.C. Code Ann. Sections 17-25-20, 17-25-30; McAninch et al., 2007).

3. Starting with the supplemental court administration list of all criminal cases that went to trial in fiscal year 2001, we successfully matched 85 percent of these (260 of 306 total trials) with the commission data. Some of the failed matches were sealed cases listed in the supplemental court administration data that might have been excluded from the commission's dataset, while other cases failed to match for unknown reasons.

4. To account for the nonuniform nature of parole eligibility for South Carolina offenses, the expected minimum sentence was chosen over other alternatives because offenders might have been eligible for parole after serving 25 percent, 33 percent, or 85 percent of their sentences or may have never been eligible, depending on the classification of the offense. Using the expected minimum rather than the imposed maximum accounted for these differences in parole eligibility (Chiricos and Bales, 1991; Gertz and Price, 1985; Spohn and Cederblom, 1991). The expected minimum was calculated by adjusting the imposed maximum sentence by a parole eligibility multiplier as determined by the controlling offense (e.g., 0.25, 0.33, 0.85, 1.0). For example, if an offender were sentenced to 10 years and fell under the 25 percent parole eligibility designation, the expected minimum would be 2.5 years ($10 \times .25$), or 30 months.

5. We were not able to discern between prison and jail sentences. Defendants sentenced to more than three months' custodial time are processed into the state correctional system; defendants given less than three months serve their time in local jails or detention centers. Thus, unlike in some states, circuit court judges do not make an independent decision of whether to send incarcerated offenders to a local jail or central prison—that decision is a product of the length of the sentence imposed.

6. Because there was evidence of overdispersion in our data, we opted to estimate the hurdle model using a zero-truncated negative binomial model for positive counts. For the HRM-NB model, we used the same set of predictors for the incarceration decision as we did for the truncated sentencing count.

7. Technically called "Bernoulli" models for their use of the Bernoulli distribution, where 1 is the success probability p and 0 is the failure probability $q = 1 - p$ (McCullagh and Nelder, 1989; Raudenbush and Bryk, 2002; Ulmer, Bader, and Gault, 2008; Wooldredge, 2010).

8. Type I errors occur when the null hypothesis is falsely rejected (Weisburd and Britt, 2007).

9. Kezar (2003, p. 397) defines elite interviews as those wherein the interviewees are known to have participated in a certain situation, in which the researcher has reviewed information necessary to arrive at a provisional analysis, where

the researcher produces an interview guide based on this analysis, and where the result of the interview is the participant's definition of the situation.

10. In addition, while some researchers prefer to tape-record interviews, others suggest not doing so. Recording seems most efficacious for person-to-person interviews as it frees the questioner from constant note-taking and helps maintain a conversational approach to the interview (Berry, 2002; Peabody et al., 1990). The decision was made to not record the interviews to ease the reluctance and potential chilling effect (see, e.g., Katz, 2001). Since they were not conducted in person, the author was able to constantly take notes without damaging rapport.

11. Of the 2,022 presumptive prison sex grid cases, downward dispositional departures were entered in 787 (26 percent) cases.

12. The offense severity levels and ranges on the sex grid differ from those on the standard grid. Accordingly, these cases could not be included in the same models.

References

Albonetti, C. A. (1991). An integration of theories to explain judicial discretion. *Social Problems*, *38*(2), 247–266.

Ashworth, A. (1995). *Sentencing and criminal justice* (2nd ed). Butterworths.

Austin, A. (2010). *Criminal justice trends: Key legislative changes in sentencing policy, 2001–2010*. Vera Institute of Justice.

Austin, J. (2010). Reducing America's correctional populations: A strategic plan. *Justice Research and Policy*, *12*(1), 9–40.

Bagaric, M. (2000). Consistency and fairness in sentencing: The splendor of fixed penalties. *California Criminal Law Review*, *2*.

Baughman, S. B. (2019). Dividing Bail Reform. *Iowa Law Review*, *105*, 947.

Baumer, E. P. (2013). Reassessing and redirecting research on race and sentencing. *Justice Quarterly*, *30*(2), 231–261.

Becker, H. S. (1998). *Tricks of the trade: How to think about your research while you're doing it*. University of Chicago Press.

Bergstrom, M., and Mistick, J. (2003). The Pennsylvania experience: Public release of judge-specific sentencing data. *Federal Sentencing Reporter*, *16*(1), 57–66.

Bernard, H. R., and Ryan, G. W. (2010). Content analysis. *Analyzing qualitative data: Systematic approaches*, *2*, 287–310.

Berry, J. M. (2002). Validity and reliability issues in elite interviewing. *PS: Political Science and Politics*, *35*(4), 679–682.

Blumer, H. (1969). *Symbolic interactionism* (Vol. 9). Prentice-Hall.

Blumstein, A., Cohen, J., Martin, S. E., and Tonry, M. H. (Eds.). (1983). *Research on sentencing: The search for reform* (Vol. 1). National Academy Press.

Boerner, D. (1985). *Sentencing in Washington: A legal analysis of the Sentencing Reform Act of 1981*. Butterworth Legal Publishers.

Bontrager, S., Bales, W., and Chiricos, T. (2005). Race, ethnicity, threat and the labeling of convicted felons. *Criminology*, 43(3), 589–622.

Brereton, D., and Casper, J. D. (1981). Does it pay to plead guilty? Differential sentencing and the functioning of criminal courts. *Law and Society Review*, 16, 45.

Britt, C. L. (2000). Social context and racial disparities in punishment decisions. *Justice Quarterly*, 17(4), 707–732.

Bushway, S. D., and Forst, B. (2013). Studying discretion in the processes that generate criminal justice sanctions. *Justice Quarterly*, 30(2), 199–222.

Calpin, J. C., Kress, J. M., and Gelman, A. M. (1982). *Sentencing guidelines: Structuring judicial discretion: Vol. 2, Analytic bases for the formulation of sentencing policy*. U.S. Department of Justice, National Institute of Justice.

Cameron, A. C., and Trivedi, P. K. (2013). *Regression analysis of count data* (Vol. 53). Cambridge University Press.

Carrow, D. M., Feins, J., Lee, B. N., and Olinger, L. (1985). *Guidelines without force: An evaluation of the multi-jurisdictional sentencing guidelines field test*. ABT Associates.

Carson, E. A. (2020). *Imprisonment rate of sentenced prisoners under the jurisdiction of state or federal correctional authorities per 100,000 U.S. residents, December 31, 1978–2019*. U.S. Bureau of Justice Statistics, National Prisoner Statistics Program. https://csat.bjs.ojp.gov/quick-tables.

Charmaz, K. (2002). Qualitative interviewing and grounded theory analysis. In J. F. Gubrium and J. A. Holstein (Eds.), *Handbook of Interview Research: Context and Method* (pp. 675–694). Sage.

Chiricos, T. G., and Bales, W. D. (1991). Unemployment and punishment: An empirical assessment. *Criminology*, 29(4), 701–724.

Clair, M., and Winter, A. S. (2016). How judges think about racial disparities: Situational decision-making in the criminal justice system. *Criminology*, 54(2), 332–359.

Clark Foundation. (2022). The Edna McConnell Clark Foundation. About us, Legacy Programs, Program for Justice. https://www.emcf.org/about-us/our-history/legacy-programs/. Visited September 28, 2022.

Clegg, S. (2012). Sociology of organizations. In G. Ritzer (Ed.), *The Wiley-Blackwell companion to sociology* (pp. 164–181). Blackwell.

Corbin, J., and Strauss, A. (2014). *Basics of qualitative research: Techniques and procedures for developing grounded theory*. Sage.

Corda, A., and Hester, R. (2021). Leaving the shining city on a hill: A plea for rediscovering comparative criminal justice policy in the United States. *International Criminal Justice Review*, 31(2), 203–223.

Creswell, J. W. (2014). *A concise introduction to mixed methods research*. Sage.

Crooks, D. J. (2015). Crash course in South Carolina sentencing law—release dates, and credits, and sentencing sheets: Oh my! *South Carolina Lawyer Magazine*, 27(1), 40.

Crow, M. S., and Gertz, M. (2008). Sentencing policy and disparity: Guidelines and the influence of legal and democratic subcultures. *Journal of Criminal Justice, 36*(4), 362–371.

D'Alessio, S. J., and Stolzenberg, L. (1997). The effect of available capacity on jail incarceration: An empirical test of Parkinson's law. *Journal of Criminal Justice, 25*(4), 279–288.

Daly, K. (1989). Rethinking judicial paternalism: Gender, work-family relations, and sentencing. *Gender and Society, 3*(1), 9–36.

Davis, K. C. (1969). *Discretionary justice: A preliminary inquiry.* Louisiana State University Press.

Demuth, S., and Steffensmeier, D. (2004). Ethnicity effects on sentence outcomes in large urban courts: Comparisons among white, Black, and Hispanic defendants. *Social Science Quarterly, 85*(4), 994–1011.

Deutschmann, D. D., and Benjamin, S. K. (2000). Accurately advising clients on parole eligibility. *South Carolina Lawyer, 12*, 26–30.

Diamond, S. S., and Zeisel, H. (1975). Sentencing councils: A study of sentence disparity and its reduction. *University of Chicago Law Review, 43*, 109–149.

DiMaggio, P. J., and Powell, W. W. (1983). The iron cage revisited: Institutional isomorphism and collective rationality in organizational fields. *American Sociological Review, 48*(2), 147–160.

Dixon, J. (1995). The organizational context of criminal sentencing. *American Journal of Sociology, 100*(5), 1157–1198.

Doyle, R. F. (1961). A sentencing council in operation. *Federal Probation, 25*, 27–30.

Dunlea, R. R. (2022). "No idea whether he's Black, white, or purple": Colorblindness and cultural scripting in prosecution. *Criminology, 60*(2), 237–262.

Eisenstein, J., Flemming, R. B., and Nardulli, P. F. (1988). *The contours of justice: Communities and their courts.* Little, Brown.

Eisenstein, J., and Jacob, H. (1977). *Felony justice: An organizational analysis of criminal courts.* Little, Brown.

Ellenberg, J. (2021). *Shape: The hidden geometry of information, biology, strategy, democracy, and everything else.* Penguin.

Enders, C. K., and Tofighi, D. (2007). Centering predictor variables in cross-sectional multilevel models: A new look at an old issue. *Psychological Methods, 12*(2), 121–138.

Engen, R. L. (2009). Assessing determinate and presumptive sentencing: Making research relevant. *Criminology and Public Policy, 8*, 323.

Engen, R. L., Gainey, R. R., Crutchfield, R. D., and Weis, J. G. (2003). Discretion and disparity under sentencing guidelines: The role of departures and structured sentencing alternatives. *Criminology, 41*(1), 99–130.

Engen, R. L., and Steen, S. (2000). The power to punish: Discretion and sentencing reform in the war on drugs. *American Journal of Sociology, 105*(5), 1357–1395.

Fearn, N. (2005). A multilevel analysis of community effects on criminal sentencing. *Justice Quarterly, 22*, 452–487.

Feeley, M. M. (1979). *The process is the punishment: Handling cases in a lower criminal court*. Russell Sage Foundation.

Feeley, M. M., and Simon, J. (1992). The new penology: Notes on the emerging strategy of corrections and its implications. *Criminology, 30*(4), 449–474.

Feld, B. C. (1991). Justice by geography: Urban, suburban, and rural variations in juvenile justice administration. *Journal of Criminal Law and Criminology, 82*, 156.

Fischman, J. B., and Schanzenbach, M. M. (2012). Racial disparities under the federal sentencing guidelines: The role of judicial discretion and mandatory minimums. *Journal of Empirical Legal Studies, 9*(4), 729–764.

Flemming, R. B., Nardulli, P. F., and Eisenstein, J. (1992). *The craft of justice: Politics and work in criminal court communities*. University of Pennsylvania Press.

Francis, J. J., Johnston, M., Robertson, C., Glidewell, L., Entwistle, V., Eccles, M. P., and Grimshaw, J. M. (2010). What is an adequate sample size? Operationalising data saturation for theory-based interview studies. *Psychology and Health, 25*(10), 1229–1245.

Frankel, M. E. (1973). *Criminal sentences: Law without order*. Hill and Wang.

Frase, R. S. (1994). State sentencing guidelines: Still going strong. *Judicature, 78*, 173–179.

———. (2009). What explains persistent racial disproportionality in Minnesota's prison and jail populations? *Crime and Justice, 38*(1), 201–280.

———. (2013). *Just sentencing: Principles and procedures for a workable system*. Oxford University Press.

———. (2017). Examining the operation and impacts of prior record sentencing enhancements. *Federal Sentencing Reporter, 30*(1), 74–79.

———. (2019). Forty years of American sentencing guidelines: What have we learned? *Crime and Justice, 48*(1), 79–135.

Frase, R. S., and Hester, R. (2019). Disproportionate impacts on minority offenders. In R. S. Frase and J. V. Roberts (Eds.), *Paying for the past: The case against prior record sentence enhancements* (pp. 128–152). Oxford University Press.

Frase, R. S., and Mitchell, K. L. (2019). Sentencing guidelines in the United States. In C. Spohn and P. Brennan (Eds.), *Handbook on sentencing policies and practices in the 21st century* (pp. 43–67). Routledge.

Frase, R. S., and Roberts, J. V. (2019). *Paying for the past: The case against prior record sentence enhancements*. Oxford University Press.

Frase, R. S., Roberts, J., Hester, R., and Mitchell, K. L. (2015). *Criminal history enhancements sourcebook*. Robina Institute of Criminal Law and Criminal Justice.

Frazier, C. E., and Bock, E. W. (1982). Effects of court officials on sentence severity: Do judges make a difference? *Criminology, 20*(2), 257–272.

Freiburger, T. L., and Hilinski, C. M. (2013). An examination of the interactions of race and gender on sentencing decisions using a trichotomous dependent variable. *Crime and Delinquency, 59*(1), 59–86.

Garland, D. (1993). *Punishment and modern society: A study in social theory*. University of Chicago Press.
———. (2000). The culture of high crime societies. *British Journal of Criminology*, 40(3), 347–375.
———. (2009). A culturalist theory of punishment? Punishment and culture, Philip Smith. Chicago, IL: University of Chicago Press, 2008. 183 pp. $19.00 (pbk). ISBN 9780226766102. *Punishment and Society*, 11(2), 259–268.
———. (2012). *The culture of control: Crime and social order in contemporary society*. University of Chicago Press.
Gertz, M. G., and Price, A. C. (1985). Variables influencing sentencing severity: Intercourt differences in Connecticut. *Journal of Criminal Justice*, 13(2), 131–139.
Ghent, R. D. (1998). State sentencing guidelines: The case against them. *South Carolina Lawyer*, 9(5), 43.
Goldstein, K. (2002). Getting in the door: Sampling and completing elite interviews. *PS: Political Science and Politics*, 35(4), 669–672.
Gottfredson, D. M., and Ballard, K. B. (1965). *The validity of two parole prediction scales: An eight year follow up study*. California Medical Facility.
Gottfredson, D. M., and Beverly, R. F. (1962). *Development and operational use of prediction methods in correctional work*. Institute for the Study of Crime and Delinquency.
Gottfredson, D. M., Hoffman, P. B., Sigler, M. H., and Wilkins, L. T. (1975). Making paroling policy explicit. *Crime and Delinquency*, 21(1), 34–44.
Gottfredson, D. M., Wilkins, L. T., and Hoffman, P. B. (1978). *Guidelines for parole and sentencing: A policy control method*. Lexington Books.
Gruhl, J., Spohn, C., and Welch, S. (1981). Women as policymakers: The case of trial judges. *American Journal of Political Science*, 25(2), 308–322.
Guerino, P., Harrison, P. M., and Sabol, W. L. (2012). *Prisoners in 2010*. U.S. Department of Justice, Bureau of Justice Statistics.
Guest, G., Bunce, A., and Johnson, L. (2006). How many interviews are enough? An experiment with data saturation and variability. *Field methods*, 18(1), 59–82.
Harmon, M. G. (2013). "Fixed" sentencing: The effect on imprisonment rates over time. *Journal of Quantitative Criminology*, 29, 369–397.
Harries, Keith D., and Russell Lura. (1974). The geography of justice-sentencing variations in US judicial districts. *Judicature*, 57, 392–401.
Hartley, R. D., Maddan, S., and Spohn, C. C. (2007). Concerning conceptualization and operationalization: Sentencing data and the focal concerns perspective—A research note. *Southwest Journal of Criminal Justice*, 4(1), 58–78.
Harwell-Beach, A. (1998). Pro: Sentencing reform in South Carolina—The return of sentencing guidelines. *South Carolina Lawyer*, 42–44.
Hester, R. (2012). Criminal sentencing in the court communities of South Carolina: An examination of offender, judge, and county characteristics. Ph.D. dissertation. University of South Carolina.

———. (2016). Sentencing policies and practices in South Carolina (Oxford Handbooks Online). Oxford University Press.

———. (2017). Judicial rotation as centripetal force: Sentencing in the court communities of South Carolina. *Criminology*, 55(1), 205–235.

———. (2019a). Prior record and recidivism risk. *American Journal of Criminal Justice*, 44(3), 353–375.

———. (2019b). Risk Assessment at Sentencing. In J. V. Roberts, J. W. de Keijser, and J. Ryberg (Eds.), *Predictive sentencing: Normative and empirical perspectives* (p. 213). Bloomsbury Publishing.

———. (2019c). Sentencing Disparity and Mass Incarceration. In V. A. Edkins and A. D. Redlich (Eds.), *A system of pleas: Social sciences contributions to the real legal system* (pp. 153–167). Oxford University Press.

———. (2020). Risk assessment savvy: The imperative of appreciating accuracy and outcome. *Behavioral Sciences and the Law*, 38(3), 246–258.

———. (2021). Punishing for the past (sometimes): Judicial perspectives on criminal history enhancements. *Prison Journal*, 101(4), 443–465.

Hester, R., Frase, R. S., Laskorunsky, J., and Mitchell, K. L. (2019). Rethinking the role of criminal history in sentencing. In C. Spohn and P. Brennan (Eds.), *Handbook on sentencing policies and practices in the 21st century*. Routledge.

Hester, R., Frase, R. S., Roberts, J. V., and Mitchell, K. L. (2018). Prior record enhancements at sentencing: Unsettled justifications and unsettling consequences. *Crime and Justice*, 47(1), 209–254.

Hester, R., and Hartman, T. K. (2017). Conditional race disparities in criminal sentencing: A test of the liberation hypothesis from a non-guidelines state. *Journal of Quantitative Criminology*, 33(1), 77–100.

Hester, R., Roberts, J. V., Frase, R. S., and Mitchell, K. (2018). A measure of tolerance: Public attitudes on sentencing enhancements for old and juvenile prior records. *Corrections*, 3(2), 137–151.

Hester, R., and Sevigny, E. L. (2016). Court communities in local context: A multilevel analysis of felony sentencing in South Carolina. *Journal of Crime and Justice*, 39(1), 55–74.

Hilbe, J. M. (2014). *Modeling count data*. Cambridge University Press.

Hoffman, P. B. (1972). Paroling policy feedback. *Journal of Research in Crime and Delinquency*, 9(2), 117–131.

Hoffman, P. B., and Beck, J. L. (1974). Parole decision-making: A salient factor score. *Journal of Criminal Justice*, 2(3), 195–206.

Holt, A. (2010). Using the telephone for narrative interviewing: A research note. *Qualitative Research*, 10(1), 113–121.

Hyatt, J. M., Chanenson, S. L., and Bergstrom, M. H. (2011). Reform in motion: The promise and perils of incorporating risk assessments and cost-benefit analysis into Pennsylvania sentencing. *Duquesne Law Review*, 49, 707.

Jacobs, B. A., and Wright, R. (1999). Stick-up, street culture, and offender motivation. *Criminology*, 37(1), 149–174.

Johnson, B. D. (2005). Contextual disparities in guidelines departures: Courtroom social contexts, guidelines compliance, and extralegal disparities in criminal sentencing 1. *Criminology, 43*(3), 761–796.

———. (2006). The multilevel context of criminal sentencing: Integrating judge- and county-level influences. *Criminology, 44*(2), 259–298.

———. (2012). Cross-classified multilevel models: An application to the criminal case processing of indicted terrorists. *Journal of Quantitative Criminology, 28*(1), 163–189.

Johnson, B. D., Ulmer, J. T., and Kramer, J. H. (2008). The social context of guidelines circumvention: The case of federal district courts. *Criminology, 46*(3), 737–783.

Kahneman, D. (2011). *Thinking, fast and slow.* Macmillan.

Katz, J. (2001). From how to why: On luminous description and causal inference in ethnography (Part I). *Ethnography, 2*(4), 443–473.

Kautt, P. M. (2002). Location, location, location: Interdistrict and intercircuit variation in sentencing outcomes for federal drug-trafficking offenses. *Justice Quarterly, 19*(4), 633–671.

Kautt, P. M., and DeLone, M. A. (2006). Sentencing outcomes under competing but coexisting sentencing interventions: Untying the Gordian knot. *Criminal Justice Review, 31*(2), 105–131.

Kezar, A. (2003). Transformational elite interviews: Principles and problems. *Qualitative inquiry, 9*(3), 395–415.

Kim, B., Spohn, C., and Hedberg, E. C. (2015). Federal sentencing as a complex collaborative process: Judges, prosecutors, judge-prosecutor dyads, and disparity in sentencing. *Criminology, 53*(4), 597–623.

King, N. J., Soulé, D. A., Steen, S., and Weidner, R. R. (2005). When process affects punishment: Differences in sentences after guilty plea, bench trial, and jury trial in five guidelines states. *Columbia Law Review, 105*, 959.

King, R. D. (2019). Cumulative impact: Why prison sentences have increased. *Criminology, 57*(1), 157–180.

King, R. D., and Light, M. T. (2019). Have racial and ethnic disparities in sentencing declined? *Crime and Justice, 48*(1), 365–437.

Knapp, K. A. (1982). Impact of the Minnesota sentencing guidelines on sentencing practices. *Hamline Law Review, 5*, 237.

———. (1993). Allocation of discretion and accountability within sentencing structures. *University of Colorado Law Review, 64*(3), 679.

Koons-Witt, B. A., Sevigny, E. L., Burrow, J. D., and Hester, R. (2014). Gender and sentencing outcomes in South Carolina: Examining the interactions with race, age, and offense type. *Criminal Justice Policy Review, 25*(3), 299–324.

Kramer, J. H., and Ulmer, J. T. (2002). Downward departures for serious violent offenders: Local court "corrections" to Pennsylvania's sentencing guidelines. *Criminology, 40*(4), 897–932.

———. (2009). *Sentencing guidelines: Lessons from Pennsylvania.* Lynne Rienner.

Kritzer, H. M., and Uhlman, T. M. (1977). Sisterhood in the courtroom: Sex of judge and defendant as factors in criminal case disposition. *Social Science Journal*, *14*(2), 77–88.

Kurlychek, M. C., and Johnson, B. D. (2019). Cumulative disadvantage in the American criminal justice system. *Annual Review of Criminology*, *2*(1), 291–319.

Kutateladze, B. L., Andiloro, N. R., and Johnson, B. D. (2016). Opening Pandora's box: How does defendant race influence plea bargaining? *Justice Quarterly*, *33*(3), 398–426.

Kutateladze, B. L., Andiloro, N. R., Johnson, B. D., and Spohn, C. C. (2014). Cumulative disadvantage: Examining racial and ethnic disparity in prosecution and sentencing. *Criminology*, *52*(3), 514–551.

Kuzel, A.J. (1992). Sampling in qualitative inquiry. In B. F. Crabtree and W. L. Miller (Eds.), *Doing qualitative research* (pp. 31–44). Sage.

Kvale, S., and Brinkmann, S. (2009). *Interviews: Learning the craft of qualitative research interviewing*. Sage.

Lappi-Seppälä, T. (2011). Sentencing and punishment in Finland: The decline of the repressive ideal. In M. Tonry (Ed.), *Why punish? How much? A reader on punishment* (pp. 239–254). Oxford University Press.

Levin, M. A. (1972). *Urban politics and policy outcomes: The criminal courts*. Wadsworth.

Long, J. S. (1997). *Regression models for categorical and limited dependent variables: Advanced quantitative techniques in the social sciences* (Vol. 7). Sage.

Lynch, M. (2019). Focally concerned about focal concerns: A conceptual and methodological critique of sentencing disparities research. *Justice Quarterly*, *36*(7), 1148–1175.

Lynch, M., and Bertenthal, A. (2016). The calculus of the record: Criminal history in the making of US federal sentencing guidelines. *Theoretical Criminology*, *20*(2), 145–164.

Maguire, K., and Flanagan, T. J. (1990). *Sourcebook of criminal justice statistics: 1990*. U.S. Department of Justice, Bureau of Justice Statistics.

Martinson, R. (1974). What works? Questions and answers about prison reform. *Public Interest*, *35*, 22.

Marvell, T., and Moody, C. (1996). Determinate sentencing and abolishing parole: The long-term impact on prisons and crime. *Criminology*, *34*(1), 107–128.

Mauer, M., and Ghandnoosh, N. (2013, Dec. 20; updated Dec. 6, 2017). Can we wait 88 years to end mass incarceration? *Huffington Post*. https://www.huffpost.com/entry/88-years-mass-incarceration_b_4474132.

Mayson, S. G. (2019). Detention by any other name. *Duke Law Journal*, *69*, 1643.

McAninch, W. S., Fairey, W. G., and Coggiola, L. M. (2013). *The criminal law of South Carolina*. South Carolina Bar, Continuing Legal Education.

McCullagh, P., and Nelder, J. A. (1989). *Generalized linear models*. Chapman and Hall.

McCulley, M. G. (1999). *Drug litigation in South Carolina*. South Carolina Bar.
Metcalfe, C. (2016). The role of courtroom workgroups in felony case dispositions: An analysis of workgroup familiarity and similarity. *Law and Society Review, 50*(3), 637–673.
Minnesota Sentencing Guidelines Commission. (1980). *Report to the legislature, January 1, 1980*, 5.
———. (2022). *Minnesota sentencing guidelines and commentary*. https://mn.gov/sentencing-guidelines/assets/1August2022MinnSentencingGuidelinesCommentary_tcm30-536102.pdf.
Mitchell, O. (2005). A meta-analysis of race and sentencing research: Explaining the inconsistencies. *Journal of Quantitative Criminology, 21*, 439–466.
Mitchell, O., Cochran, J. C., Mears, D. P., and Bales, W. D. (2017). Examining prison effects on recidivism: A regression discontinuity approach. *Justice Quarterly, 34*, 571–596.
Mullins, C. W., Wright, R., and Jacobs, B. A. (2004). Gender, streetlife and criminal retaliation. *Criminology, 42*(4), 911–940.
Myers, M., and Talarico, S. M. (1987). *The social contexts of criminal sentencing*. Springer-Verlag.
Nardulli, P. F., Eisenstein, J., and Flemming, R. B. (1988). *The tenor of justice: Criminal courts and the guilty plea process*. University of Illinois Press.
O'Reilly, M., and Parker, N. (2013). "Unsatisfactory Saturation": A critical exploration of the notion of saturated sample sizes in qualitative research. *Qualitative research, 13*(2), 190–197.
Ostrom, B. J., Ostrom, C. W., Hanson, R. A., and Kleiman, M. (2008). *Assessing consistency and fairness in sentencing: A comparative study in three states*. National Center for State Courts.
Parent, D. G. (1988). *Structuring criminal sentences: The evolution of Minnesota's sentencing guidelines*. Butterworth Legal Publishers
Peabody, R. L., Hammond, S. W., Torcom, J., Brown, L. P., Thompson, C., and Kolodny, R. (1990). Interviewing political elites. *PS: Political Science and Politics, 23*(3), 451–455.
Pennsylvania Commission on Sentencing. (2023). 8th edition guidelines. https://pcs.la.psu.edu/guidelines-statutes/sentencing/comprehensive-review-of-sentencing-guidelines/. Visited November 27, 2023.
Petersilia, J., and Cullen, F. T. (2014). Liberal but not stupid: Meeting the promise of downsizing prisons. *Stanford Journal of Criminal Law and Policy, 2*, 1–41.
Petersilia, J., and Reitz, K. R. (Eds.). (2012). *The Oxford handbook of sentencing and corrections*. Oxford University Press.
Pfaff, J. F. (2006). The continued vitality of structured sentencing following Blakely: The effectiveness of voluntary guidelines. *UCLA Law Review, 54*, 235–307.
Piehl, A. M., and Bushway, S. D. (2007). Measuring and explaining charge bargaining. *Journal of Quantitative Criminology, 23*(2), 105–125.
Rachlinski, J. J., Johnson, S. L., Wistrich, A. J., and Guthrie, C. (2009). Does unconscious racial bias affect trial judges. *Notre Dame Law Review, 84*, 1195–1246.

Rachlinski, J. J., and Wistrich, A. J. (2017). Judging the judiciary by the numbers: Empirical research on judges. *Annual Review of Law and Social Science, 13*, 17–32.

Raudenbush, S. W., and Bryk, A. S. (2002). *Hierarchical linear models: Applications and data analysis methods* (Vol. 1). Sage.

Rehavi, M. M., and Starr, S. B. (2014). Racial disparity in federal criminal sentences. *Journal of Political Economy, 122*(6), 1320–1354.

Reitz, K. R. (1998). Modeling discretion in American sentencing systems. *Law and Policy, 20*(4), 389–428.

———. (2005). Don't blame determinacy: US incarceration growth has been driven by other forces. *Texas Law Review, 84*, 1787.

———. (2009). Demographic impact statements, O'Connor's warning, and the mysteries of prison release: Topics from a sentencing reform agenda. *Florida Law Review, 61*, 683.

———. (2012). The "traditional" indeterminate sentencing model. In J. Petersilia and K. R. Reitz (Eds.), *The Oxford handbook of sentencing and corrections* (pp. 270–298). Oxford University Press.

Reitz, K. R., Griffith, M., and Rhine, E. E. (2023). *Prison-release discretion and prison population size: State report; South Carolina*. Robina Institute of Criminal Law and Criminal Justice.

Reitz, K. R., and Klingele, C. M. (2019). Model penal code: Sentencing—Workable limits on mass punishment. *Crime and Justice, 48*(1), 255–311.

Rhine, Edward. (2012). The present status and future prospects of parole boards and parole supervision. In *The Oxford Handbook of Sentencing and Corrections*. https://doi.org/10.1093/oxfordhb/9780199730148.013.0026.

Richards, M. S. (1986). *South Carolina Sentencing Guidelines Commission: Final report*. South Carolina Sentencing Guidelines Commission.

Richardson, R., and Kutateladze, B. L. (2021). Tempering expectations: A qualitative study of prosecutorial reform. *Journal of Research in Crime and Delinquency, 58*(1), 41–73.

Ridgeway, G., Moyer, R. A., and Bushway, S. D. (2020). Sentencing scorecards: Reducing racial disparities in prison sentences at their source. *Criminology and Public Policy, 19*(4), 1113–1138.

Roberts, J. V. (2019). The evolution of sentencing guidelines in Minnesota and England and Wales. *Crime and Justice, 48*(1), 187–253.

———. (2020). The time of punishment: Proportionality and the sentencing of historic crimes. https://papers.ssrn.com/sol3/papers.cfm?abstract_id=3894262.

Roberts, J. V., and Sanchez, J. P. (2015). Paying for the past: The role of previous convictions at sentencing in the Crown Court. In *Exploring sentencing practice in England and Wales* (pp. 154–172). Palgrave Macmillan.

Roberts, J. V., and von Hirsch, A. (Eds.). (2010). *Previous convictions at sentencing: Theoretical and applied perspectives*. Bloomsbury Publishing.

Robina Institute of Criminal Law and Criminal Justice. (n.d.). Sentencing Guidelines Resource Center. https://robinainstitute.umn.edu/sentencing-guidelines-resource-center. Visited September 28, 2022.

Rodriguez, S. F., Curry, T. R., and Lee, G. (2006). Gender differences in criminal sentencing: Do effects vary across violent, property, and drug offenses? *Social Science Quarterly*, 87(2), 318–339.

Rothman, D. J. (1980). Conscience and convenience: The asylum and its alternatives in progressive America. *Michigan Law Review*, 79, 916.

Roulston, K. (2010). Considering quality in qualitative interviewing. *Qualitative research*, 10(2), 199–228.

———. (2014). Interactional problems in research interviews. *Qualitative Research*, 14(3), 277–293.

Saltzman, E. W., and Ulbrich, H. H. (2006). *Revenue and the South Carolina budget, 2006 December*. Strom Thurmond Institute of Government and Public Affairs.

Santos Silva, J. M. C., and Tenreyo, S. (2006). The log of gravity. *Review of Economics and Statistics*, 88(4), 641–658.

Schauffler, R. Y., LaFountain, R. C., Strickland, S. M., and Raftery, W. E. (2006). *Examining the work of state courts, 2005: A national perspective from the court statistics project*. National Center for State Courts.

Scott, W. R. (2013). *Institutions and organizations: Ideas, interests, and identities*. Sage.

Segal, J. A., and Spaeth, H. J. (2002). *The Supreme Court and the attitudinal model revisited*. Cambridge University Press.

Shah, A. K., and Oppenheimer, D. M. (2008). Heuristics made easy: An effort-reduction framework. *Psychological Bulletin*, 134(2), 207.

Siegel, A. (2005). When prosecutors control criminal court dockets: Dispatches on history and policy from a land time forgot. *American Journal of Criminal Law*, 32, 325.

Silva, J. S., and Tenreyro, S. (2006). The log of gravity. *Review of Economics and Statistics*, 88(4), 641–658.

Silverman, D. (2013). *Doing qualitative research: A practical handbook*. Sage.

Smigel, E. O. (1958). Interviewing a legal elite: The Wall Street lawyer. *American Journal of Sociology*, 64(2), 159–164.

South Carolina Department of Corrections. (2023). Department of Corrections History. https://www.doc.sc.gov/about_scdc/AgencyHistory1.pdf. Visited June 22, 2023.

South Carolina Department of Probation, Parole, and Pardon Services. (2012). *Accountability Report 2012*.

———. (2022). https://www.dppps.sc.gov/. Visited September 28, 2022.

South Carolina Sentencing Guidelines Commission. (1991). *Annual accountability report*.

———. (1997). *Annual accountability report*.

——. (2001). *Truth in sentencing: Advisory sentencing guidelines and criminal justice plan.*

——. (n.d.). *History, crime classification, truth in sentencing, and sentencing guidelines.*

South Carolina Sentencing Reform Commission. (2010). *Report to the General Assembly.* http://www.scstatehouse.gov/citizensinterestpage/SentencingReformCommission/CombinedFinalReport020110SigPage.pdf.

Spiegelhalter, D. (2019). *The art of statistics: Learning from data.* Penguin UK.

Spohn, C. (1990). The sentencing decisions of Black and white judges: Expected and unexpected similarities. *Law and Society Review, 24*(5), 1197–1216.

——. (2000). Thirty years of sentencing reform: The quest for a racially neutral sentencing process. In *Criminal justice 2000: Politics, processes, and decisions of the criminal justice system* (pp. 427–501). National Institute of Justice/National Criminal Justice Reference Service.

——. (2009). *How do judges decide? The search for justice and fairness in punishment* (2nd ed.). Sage.

Spohn, C., and Cederblom, J. (1991). Race and disparities in sentencing: A test of the liberation hypothesis. *Justice Quarterly, 8*(3), 305–327.

Spohn, C., and DeLone, M. (2000). When does race matter? An analysis of the conditions under which race affects sentence severity. *Sociology of Crime, Law, and Deviance, 2*(1), 3–37.

Spohn, C., and Holleran, D. (2000). The imprisonment penalty paid by young, unemployed Black and Hispanic male offenders. *Criminology, 38*(1), 281–306.

Steffensmeier, D. J. (1980). Assessing the impact of the women's movement on sex-based differences in the handling of adult criminal defendants. *Crime and Delinquency, 26*(3), 344–357.

Steffensmeier, D., and Britt, C. L. (2001). Judges' race and judicial decision making: Do Black judges sentence differently? *Social Science Quarterly, 82*(4), 749–764.

Steffensmeier, D., and Demuth, S. (2000). Ethnicity and sentencing outcomes in US federal courts: Who is punished more harshly? *American Sociological Review, 65*(5), 705–729.

——. (2001). Ethnicity and judges' sentencing decisions: Hispanic-Black-white comparisons. *Criminology, 39*(1), 145–178.

Steffensmeier, D. J., and Faulkner, G. L. (1978). Defendant's parental status as affecting judges' behavior: An experimental test. *Psychological Reports, 42*(3), 939–945.

Steffensmeier, D., and Hebert, C. (1999). Women and men policymakers: Does the judge's gender affect the sentencing of criminal defendants? *Social Forces, 77*(3), 1163–1196.

Steffensmeier, D., Kramer, J., and Streifel, C. (1993). Gender and imprisonment decisions. *Criminology, 31*(3), 411–446.

Steffensmeier D., and Painter-Davis, N. (2018). Focal concerns theory as conceptual tool for studying intersectionality in sentencing disparities: Focus on gender and race along with age. In J. T. Ulmer J. T. and M. S. Bradley (Eds.),

Handbook on punishment decisions: Locations of disparity (pp. 189–210). Routledge.

Steffensmeier, D. J., and Terry, R. M. (1973). Deviance and respectability: An observational study of reactions to shoplifting. *Social Forces, 51*(4), 417–426.

Steffensmeier, D., Ulmer, J., and Kramer, J. (1998). The interaction of race, gender, and age in criminal sentencing: The punishment cost of being young, Black, and male. *Criminology, 36*(4), 763–798.

Steiner, B. (2009). The effects of juvenile transfer to criminal court on incarceration decisions. *Justice Quarterly, 26*(1), 77–106.

Stemen, D., Rengifo, A., and Wilson, J. (2005). *Of fragmentation and ferment: The impact of state sentencing policies on incarceration rates, 1975–2002.* Vera Institute of Justice.

Stephens, N. (2007). Collecting data from elites and ultra elites: Telephone and face-to-face interviews with macroeconomists. *Qualitative Research, 7*(2), 203–216.

Stith, K., and Cabranes, J. A. (1998). *Fear of judging: Sentencing guidelines in the federal courts.* University of Chicago Press.

Stolzenberg, L., and D'Alessio, S. J. (1994). Sentencing and unwarranted disparity: An empirical assessment of the long-term impact of sentencing guidelines in Minnesota. *Criminology, 32*(2), 301–310.

Sudnow, D. (1965). Normal crimes: Sociological features of the penal code in a public defender office. *Social Problems, 12*(3), 255–276.

Toliver, L. J., and Brown, L. O. B. (1974). *Sentencing and the law and order syndrome in South Carolina.* South Carolina Council for Human Rights.

Tonry, M. (1992). Mandatory penalties. *Crime and Justice, 16,* 243–273.

———. (1993). Sentencing commissions and their guidelines. *Crime and Justice, 17,* 137–195.

———. (1996). *Sentencing matters.* Oxford University Press.

———. (2006). Purposes and functions of sentencing. *Crime and Justice, 34*(1), 1–53.

———. (2010a). The social, psychological, and political causes of racial disparities in the American criminal justice system. *Crime and Justice, 39*(1), 273–312.

———. (Ed.). (2010b). *Why punish? How much?: A reader on punishment.* Oxford University Press.

———. (2013). Sentencing in America, 1975–2025. *Crime and Justice, 42*(1), 141–198.

———. (2016). *Sentencing fragments: Penal reform in America, 1975–2025.* Oxford University Press.

Travis, J., Western, B., and Redburn, F. S. (2014). *The growth of incarceration in the United States: Exploring causes and consequences.* National Academies Press.

Ulmer, J. T. (1997). *Social worlds of sentencing: Court communities under sentencing guidelines.* SUNY Press.

———. (2012). Recent developments and new directions in sentencing research. *Justice Quarterly, 29*(1), 1–40.

———. (2019). Criminal courts as inhabited institutions: Making sense of difference and similarity in sentencing. *Crime and Justice*, *48*(1), 483–522.

Ulmer, J. T., Bader, C., and Gault, M. (2008). Do moral communities play a role in criminal sentencing? Evidence from Pennsylvania. *Sociological Quarterly*, *49*(4), 737–768.

Ulmer, J. T., and Bradley, M. S. (2006). Variation in trial penalties among serious violent offenses. *Criminology*, *44*(3), 631–670.

Ulmer, J. T., and Johnson, B. (2004). Sentencing in context: A multilevel analysis. *Criminology*, *42*(1), 137–178.

Ulmer, J. T., and Johnson, B. D. (2017). Organizational conformity and punishment. *Journal of Criminal Law and Criminology (1973–)*, *107*(2), 253–292.

Ulmer, J. T., and Kramer, J. H. (1996). Court communities under sentencing guidelines: Dilemmas of formal rationality and sentencing disparity. *Criminology*, *34*(3), 383–408.

———. (1998). The use and transformation of formal decision-making criteria: Sentencing guidelines, organizational contexts, and case processing strategies. *Social Problems*, *45*(2), 248–267.

Ulmer, J. T., Painter-Davis, N., and Tinik, L. (2016). Disproportional imprisonment of Black and Hispanic males: Sentencing discretion, processing outcomes, and policy structures. *Justice Quarterly*, *33*(4), 642–681.

U.S. Census Bureau. (2001, August). *Census 2000 brief: The Black population; 2000* (Report No. C2KBR/01-5). Retrieved from https://www2.census.gov/library/publications/decennial/2000/briefs/c2kbr01-05.pdf.

Van Cleve, N. G. (2016). *Crook county: Racism and injustice in America's largest criminal court*. Stanford University Press.

von Hirsch, A. (1976). *Doing justice: The choice of punishments*. Hill and Wang.

———. (2010). Proportionality and progressive loss of mitigation: Further reflections. In J. V. Roberts and A. von Hirsch (Eds.), *Previous convictions at sentencing: Theoretical and applied perspectives* (pp. 1–16). Hart Publishing.

Wang, X., and Mears, D. P. (2010). A multilevel test of minority threat effects on sentencing. *Journal of Quantitative Criminology*, *26*(2), 191–215.

———. (2015). Sentencing and state-level racial and ethnic contexts. *Law and Society Review*, *49*(4), 883–915.

Wang, X., Mears, D. P., Spohn, C., and Dario, L. (2013). Assessing the differential effects of race and ethnicity on sentence outcomes under different sentencing systems. *Crime and Delinquency*, *59*(1), 87–114.

Weisberg, R. (2007). How sentencing commissions turned out to be a good idea. *Berkeley Journal of Criminal Law*, *12*, 179.

———. (2012). The sentencing commission model, 1970s to present. In J. Petersilia and K. R. Reitz (Eds.), *The Oxford handbook of sentencing and corrections* (p. 299). Oxford University Press.

Weisburd, D., and Britt, C. (2007). *Statistics in criminal justice*. Springer.

Welch, S., Combs, M., and Gruhl, J. (1988). Do Black judges make a difference? *American Journal of Political Science*, *32*(1), 126–136.

Welch, S., and Spohn, C. (1986). Evaluating the impact of prior record on judges' sentencing decisions: A seven-city comparison. *Justice Quarterly, 3,* 389.

Wilkins, D. (2015). Personal communication with the author, June 5.

Wilkins, L. T., Kress, J. M., Gottfredson, D. M., Calpin, J. C., and Gelman, A. M. (1978). *Sentencing guidelines: Structuring judicial discretion.* National Institute of Law Enforcement and Criminal Justice, Law Enforcement Assistance Administration, U.S. Department of Justice.

Willis, J. J., Mastrofski, S. D., and Weisburd, D. (2007). Making sense of COMP-STAT: A theory-based analysis of organizational change in three police departments. *Law and Society Review, 41*(1), 147–188.

Wilson, J. Q. (1975). *Thinking about crime.* Vintage.

Wooldredge, J. (2007). Neighborhood effects on felony sentencing. *Journal of Research in Crime and Delinquency, 44*(2), 238–263.

———. (2010). Judges' unequal contributions to extralegal disparities in imprisonment. *Criminology, 48*(2), 539–567.

Wooldredge, J., Griffin, T., and Pratt, T. (2001). Considering hierarchical models for research on inmate behavior: Predicting misconduct with multilevel data. *Justice Quarterly, 18*(1), 203–231.

Wooldredge, J., Griffin, T., and Rauschenberg, F. (2005). Sentencing reform and reductions in the disparate treatment of felony defendants. *Law and Society Review, 39,* 844–845.

Worden, A. P. (1995). The judge's role in plea bargaining: An analysis of judges' agreement with prosecutors' sentencing recommendations. *Justice Quarterly, 12*(2), 257–278.

Wright, R. F. (2017). Reinventing American prosecution systems. *Crime and Justice, 46*(1), 395–439.

Wright, R. F., and Levine, K. L. (2014). The cure for young prosecutors' syndrome. *Arizona Law Review, 56,* 1065–1128.

Zatz, M. S. (1987). The changing forms of racial/ethnic biases in sentencing. *Journal of Research in Crime and Delinquency, 24*(1), 69–92.

Index

Age, 38–39, 42–45, 49, 60, 66, 88, 94, 133
Albany method, 85
Appellate courts, 109
Aristotelian maxim, 5, 9, 99, 110, 130
Attitudes, 13, 34–35, 54, 60, 108

Black (African American), 31, 33, 38–39, 42–45, 48–49, 59, 79, 132–133
Blameworthiness, 7, 32–33, 51–52, 93
Budgetary constraints, 12

Caseload burdens, 17
Chanenson, Steve, 113, 145
Charge reductions, 87, 121
Circuit courts, 17, 19–20, 22, 118, 131, 139, 145–146
Cities, 75, 83, 113
Coercive isomorphism, 8, 111
Commission. *See* Sentencing commissions
Commitment score, 38, 42, 44, 132–133
COMPAS risk assessment tool, 26

Confederate flag, 55
Contours of Justice, 36
Councils, 112–113, 145
County: caseload, 48, 55, 134; effects on sentencing, 30, 34–37, 42, 44–48, 54–60, 70–71; nested models, 135; political makeup, 56; sentencing variation, 55, 73, 75, 140; wealthy, 69
Courtroom workgroup, 27, 34–36, 56, 74–78
Courts as communities theory, 7, 9, 28, 30, 34, 36, 46, 55, 73, 77, 118, 135
Crack cocaine, 26, 70
Crime rates, 13, 53
Crime reclassification, 20, 22, 23
Criminal history: criminal history score, 6, 84, 94, 99, 102, 104, 141; prior record, 2, 21, 33, 37, 79, 80–81, 132; prior record score (PRS), 6, 53, 81, 96–97
Cross-pollination, 57, 61, 67–68
Cultural norms, 69
Cumulative disadvantage, 122

Defense attorneys, 34, 49, 62–63, 73–74, 118, 121, 123, 139, 145
Departures from guidelines, 9, 99–109, 124–125, 140–141, 144, 147, 151, 155
Department of Corrections (DOC), 16, 27
Docket, 17
Drugs: possession, 26, 38, 72, 133; trafficking, 15, 70, 132; war on drugs, 13–14, 18

Economic collapse, 12
Edna McConnell Clark Foundation, 24
Eligible for parole, 14–16, 146
Environmental factors, 30, 56

FBI Uniform Crime Reports, 47
Federal sentencing guidelines. *See* Sentencing guidelines
Focal concerns theory, 7, 9, 30–34
Frankel, Marvin, 2, 13, 98, 105–106
Frase, Richard, 4–6, 52–54, 81, 95–96, 99, 115, 125
Freed, Daniel, 113

Get tough era, 13
Going rates, 35, 62, 70, 73
Good-time credit, 15–16
Gottfredson, Don M., 84–85, 87, 144
Grand mean centered, 135
Grid. *See* Matrix

Hanging judges, 61, 63–64, 74, 118
Hartman, Todd, 44, 80, 82, 133–134, 143–144
Harwell, David, 11, 15, 19–20, 22–24
Heuristics, 32, 34
Hierarchical linear models, 46–47, 134
Hirsch, Andreas von, 13, 52, 87, 95, 115

Implicit bias, 7, 33–34
Indeterminate sentencing system, 10, 13, 15
Informal local norms, 37

Inhabited institutions theory, 7, 30, 34, 36, 45, 118
Interview guide, 139, 147
Interviews, 4, 57–61, 64, 72–80, 118–122, 137–140
Isomorphism, 8, 111

Judge: characteristics, 30, 45; plea judge, 61–62, 73–74, 76, 118–119, 138; selection, 16–17, 32, 63, 126; shopping, 56, 59, 61–62, 64, 73–74, 138
Judicial discretion, 13
Judicial rotation, 6, 8–10, 16–17, 46, 56–64, 67–78, 112, 114, 118–119, 137, 139–140
Judicial system, 14, 16–17, 119, 126
Judiciary, 20, 22–24, 27, 113, 123

Lawmakers, 19, 123
Leniency, 64, 75, 90, 108
Levy, Robert, 113
Local jail, 32, 35, 89, 146
Local legal culture, 7, 30, 34, 36, 55, 57, 105–106

Magistrate courts, 145
Male, 38, 42–45, 49, 107, 133, 136, 144
Mandatory minimum, 2, 10, 14–15, 18, 38, 42, 44–45, 48, 50–51, 70, 77, 133
Master calendaring, 56, 61, 74
Matrix, 2, 51, 84–87, 102
Metropolitan, 75
Minnesota, ix, x, 3–4, 6, 9–11, 16, 20, 81, 84, 87, 94, 100, 102–107, 113, 123, 125, 140–143
Minnesota Sentencing Guidelines Commission, 11, 20, 94, 103–104, 140–141
Mitigated sentence, 52, 109
Model Penal Code on Sentencing, 96, 125, 129
Monte Carlo simulations, 134

Negative binomial model, 44, 133
Normal distribution, 107–108

Offense type, 38, 96, 104, 106, 133, 141
Omnibus Crime Reduction and Sentencing Reform Act of 2010, 25–28
Overcharging, 109
Overcrowded prison, 15

Parole: abolition, 1, 11, 14–15; board, 1, 10, 13–14, 16, 84
Pennsylvania, x, 49, 50, 53, 81, 87, 96, 99, 116, 143
Pennsylvania Commission on Sentencing, x, 81, 87, 96, 116
Pilot guidelines, 96, 116
Plea: bargaining, 17, 49, 74, 108; negotiated pleas, 17, 62–64, 66–68, 74, 139; straight pleas, 17, 63, 66–67, 74, 139
Policy reform, 11, 13
Poverty, 60, 72, 96, 109
Practical constraints, 7, 32
Pragmatic sentencers, 62, 73
Presentence investigation report, 18–19, 96, 108
Prior record. *See* Criminal history
Prison: rate, 12, 27; term, 16, 26, 40, 51, 82, 88, 90, 94, 116, 132–133
Probation, 12, 18, 26, 32, 34–35, 41, 43, 48, 51, 66, 82, 90–94, 102–103, 126, 140
Prosecutor, x, 14, 17, 22, 34, 36, 42, 45–50, 54, 57, 62–63, 68–69, 71–77, 108–109, 122–124, 127, 129, 139
Public safety, 7, 24–25, 32, 51, 93, 99
Punitiveness, 12–13, 59–60, 64–67, 108, 137–138

Qualitative research, 4, 9, 31, 45, 50, 57–60, 72–73, 77, 88, 93, 97, 108, 118–122, 136, 145, 149

Racial disparities, 2–3, 6–7, 9, 13, 30, 34, 54–55, 59, 81, 95, 99, 103, 115–117, 121–122, 136, 144
Recommended sentences, 63, 74, 79–81, 95, 100–102
Rehabilitation, 53, 66, 91
Reitz, Kevin, x, 4–5, 15–16, 28, 96, 99, 124
Remorse, 50, 128, 136
Risk assessment tool, 96
Robina Institute of Criminal Law and Criminal Justice, 4, 102

Salient Factor Score, 84, 103
Sensibilities, 13, 35, 70
Sentencing guidelines: advisory guidelines, 21–23, 82, 102, 125, 128, 143; commissions, 3–4, 6, 8, 10–13, 15, 18, 20–23, 30, 41, 60, 85, 97, 100, 103, 105, 109, 116, 123–125, 131–132, 138–139, 145; failed guidelines effort, 5, 10, 126; federal sentencing guidelines, 2, 10–11, 22, 84, 99–100, 127; formation, 94
Sentencing Reform Act of 1984, 22, 85, 113
Shoplifting, 91
Solicitor. *See* Prosecutor.
South Carolina Crime Classification Scheme, 132
South Carolina Sentencing Commission, 2–3, 11–12, 20, 131–132, 145
Standards for appellate review, 102
Statewide norms, 61, 119, 121, 138
Statewide sentencing culture, 119

Thurmond, Senator Strom, 22
Tonry, Michael, x, 1, 4, 13–14, 26, 33, 50, 52, 81, 98–99, 144
Tough-on-crime politics, 108
Traveling judges, 16, 66, 68, 138
Trial docket, 14, 61
Trial penalty, 43, 48–50, 117
Truth-in-Sentencing, 11, 14–15, 24, 27, 43, 129

U.S. Sentencing Commission, 2, 10, 12, 22, 85

Ulmer, Jeff, x, 2–4, 7–8, 31–32, 34–37, 43, 45, 47, 49–50, 56, 73, 75, 77, 79–81, 95, 103, 111, 120, 132–33, 136, 145–146
Uncertainty avoidance and causal attribution, 7, 31
Uniformity and fairness in sentencing, 2
Uniformity in sentencing, 5, 9, 19, 62, 100, 106, 123
Urban politics, 83

Violent, 16, 25, 32, 75
War on drugs, 13–14, 18
Whether or not to imprison a defendant, 40
Wilkins, David, 2, 8, 11–12, 23
Wilkins, Leslie T., 84–86
Wilkins, William W., 2, 8, 10–12, 20, 22–25, 84–86, 94, 144

Rhys Hester is Associate Professor of Sociology, Anthropology, and Criminal Justice at Clemson University.